JUDGE JOE

IN THE EYE OF THE STORM

Joe Cannon and
James Edwin Alexander

Macedon Publishing Co. : Oklahoma City

1. Joe Cannon, 1925--
2. James Edwin Alexander, 1930--

ISBN 0-939965-20-8

The paper in this book meets the guidelines for permanence and durability of the Committee on Production Guidelines for Book Longevity of the Council on Library Reources, Inc.

1 2 3 4 5 6 7 8 9 10

Contents

DEDICATION

Caroline Cannon

This book is dedicated to my beloved wife, Caroline. She and I wrote it and put it together. With the help of others, we did all the research.

We have been married forty-eight years. We have three children and six grandchildren.

She nursed me through a long and painful illness, and if it weren't for her I wouldn't be here writing this book.

Foreword

There was a time when everyone in Oklahoma knew (or knew about) Joe Cannon. At least, everyone in Oklahoma who enjoyed their evening cocktails did.

He was the crazy guy who had no more sense than to enforce Oklahoma's long scoffed-at liquor laws. He and his "prairie fire" Governor, J. Howard Edmondson, were "drying up" the state.

The year was 1959. High society places like Southern Hills Country Club, the Oklahoma City Golf and Country Club, and somewhat more accessible venues like the Chatterbox Club were raided; club employees and patrons alike were arrested and, in many cases, taken to jail for illegally serving or consuming alcoholic beverages. Roadblocks were set up, bootleggers were arrested, and lots of cases of whiskey were confiscated.

The long arm of the law fell equally on the rich and the poor, the famous and the not so well-known.

Of course, the purpose of those efforts was to make Oklahomans aware of how antiquated and silly our alcoholic beverage laws were, and to get prohibition repealed. When our new laws were enacted in 1960, it was said we moved from "liquor by the wink" to "liquor by the drink." The improbable coalition of Baptists and bootleggers who had kept Oklahoma "dry" for so many years had been overcome.

It took Joe Cannon's pressure tactics as Commissioner of Public Safety to get it done, and get it done he did. "Cannonball Joe," as the press dubbed him, had changed Oklahoma forever.

This book captures the feeling and the excitement of those days. Joe's relationship with Governor J. Howard Edmondson, who had been his law partner in their early days, brings fascinating insight into a remarkable part of our state's history.

Although I had long known about Joe, I didn't really get to know him personally until we appered in court against each other in about 1965. Joe won the case for his client. I realized that although his courtroom style may have seemed a little "rough around the edges," he was an exceptional lawyer.

We became good friends over the years and spent a lot of time together. The trips on Joe Cannon's boat, the "Okie," from Kerr Reservoir down the Arkansas River through the locks and dams to the "Light House" restaurant in Fort Smith became well known in legal/judicial circles. Many prominent judges and lawyers would join Joe and Caroline for a happy weekend.

Although the stories of Joe's encounters with President Kennedy, Frank Sinatra, and other luminaries make interesting reading, the most significant aspect of the book is its focus on Joe's judicial career and the many important cases that were tried before him. He was a fine trial judge. Of all the cases he tried, I don't believe he was ever reversed by an appellate court. Although some of his decisions were very controversial, they were always within the law.

I had a great vantage point to observe his judicial career not only as a civil practitioner in the District Courts of Oklahoma County, but I was District Attorney of Oklahoma County from 1976 to 1980. I was very much aware of several of the high-profile cases discussed in the book as they were prosecuted by my assistant district attorneys. I tried a murder case before Joe in the early days of my term of office and was impressed at his complete mastery of the applicable laws and procedures.

His judicial manner was imposing. No one in Joe's courtroom ever forgot who was in charge. He was mostly evenhanded in his rulings. I say "mostly" because it always seemed to me that he was a little bit harder on his friends who appeared before him than he was on those lawyers he did not know quite as well.

Being a friend of Joe Cannon wasn't always easy. During his years on the district court bench, he had a "running gun battle" going with someone all the time. He was almost always deeply embroiled in a controversy with various colleagues on the state court bench, judges on the federal bench, elected county officials, well-known lawyers, and even the court clerk. Not only did Joe never back away from a fight, he loved being right in the middle of one. The trouble was, he expected his friends to get right in there with him. Those of us who wanted to keep Joe for a friend, yet also had to appear in other courts before those other judges or do business with some of his opponents, sometimes had to walk a very fine line.

The thing about Joe that may not have been recognized when he first came on the bench was that he had a first-class legal mind. Joe had not been a particularly strong undergraduate student in college. But when he got to law school, he came into his own. To his surprise (and probably everyone else's) he was an outstanding law student who made really good grades! As Joe told me, "It just all seemed to make sense, and I loved it." He made one of the first "A+" grades ever recorded in the College of Law and would have been elected to the law honor society, the Order of the Coif, had he not left school to campaign for Howard Edmondson for State Representative.

His ability to read the law and analyze and remember important judicial precedents stood him well in his career on the bench. Not only did he stay ahead of most of the lawyers during his many trials, but other judges consulted him regularly on important rulings and decisions. Sometimes during the trial of an important case, when faced with an important ruling, other trial judges would declare a recess so they could "study the law." Often that "study of the law" meant a quiet phone call to Judge Cannon to get his advice. Since I knew of this tendency among certain judges, when I had a case before one of them, I would go by Joe's chambers early in the morning and discuss the law with him. It was amazing how many good rulings those judges made.

The cases described in the book were important cases with real impact on our judicial system and our society. More importantly for your purposes, they are very interesting.

Perhaps the best way to introduce this book is to describe one of Joe's political campaign ads. Joe put on one of the shortest and one of the best and most effective T.V. commercials I have ever seen. It is truly a classic. No preparation was done, no script was written, no makeup was used, no dramatic lighting was in place.

At Dale Robertson's invitation, Joe showed up at the television and movie star's farm out by El Reno one morning. Joe brought with him a cameraman. They made the commercial with one take in about five minutes. As I remember it, the commercial went like this:

> Dale Robertson is sitting on a fence, and one of his hired hands is talking to him.
>
> The hired hand says, ''I see Joe Cannon is running for reelection as a district judge. I hear he is a good judge.''
>
> Dale says, ''Listen, Joe Cannon is the finest trial judge in the United States.''
>
> The hired hand says, I didn't know that.''
>
> With his enigmatic smile, Dale says, ''Well, you know it now!''

For those of you who read the story that follows, you'll know it too!

Andrew M. Coats, Dean
University of Oklahoma Law School

"You only come this way once,
so put a little color in the game."

Preface

All my life I have followed that motto. Whether it is for that
reason or some other, the label "colorful" has been attached to
my career. Some have applied that term in a derogative manner,
as in controversial; others employ it as a mark of distinction,
denoting approval. I prefer the latter interpretation.

I never thought I would be writing a book. At least, not at this
stage of my life when I just turned seventy-six. But two sets of
circumstances have conspired to get my journalistic juices
flowing.

One set of circumstances involves the 1959 repeal of
prohibition in Oklahoma. The real story has never been told,
although many have tried. I am the only person alive who can tell
that story because I was the one who led the campaign for repeal.

The other set of circumstances concerns Governor J. Howard
Edmondson's controversial decision to have himself appointed
U.S. Senator following the January 1963 death of Robert S. Kerr.
There have been many versions told by many different people, but
no one has written the true story. How do I know? I was there. I
know exactly what happened because President John F. Kennedy
used me as a go-between in his negotiations with Edmondson. I
now welcome an opportunity to set the record straight.

Fate also had a hand in bringing me together with two people
who could make this book become a reality. Mary Pointer is my
investment advisor at Bank First who pushed me off high center
in making me tell my story. She arranged a meeting with

author/publisher James Edwin Alexander. He reviewed my materials and offered his opinion that they were worthy of publication. This is a result of that effort.

An old Chinese proverb says, "We are not responsible for the hand we are dealt in life, but we are responsible for the way we play the cards." I don't know why God served me up some of the adventures He did, or why He called upon me to do some of the things I did. I only know that my pilgrimage began in January 1925 in Muskogee, Oklahoma.

Pearl Harbor came along on the eve of my seventeenth birthday. I graduated from high school a month later and tried to join the U.S. Marines. My mother resisted at first, but ultimately relented.

I served nearly four years in the marines, two-and-a-half of them in combat in the South Pacific. Luck was with me. Despite participating in many battles, I was never wounded.

My only brother was a B-24 pilot in Europe. One day I was on beach guard duty when a messenger came up and said the commanding officer wanted to see me in his tent. The chaplain was there when I arrived. Immediately, I knew something terrible had happened. The CO said my brother was shot down in a raid over the Ploesti oil refinery in Romania and was killed.

He advised me of a new humanitarian policy the military had adopted. They wanted to avoid wiping out a whole family name, as happened when the five Sullivan brothers all perished with their ship, the cruiser USS *Juneau*. He said, "As the sole surviving son, you are entitled to return to the United States. It's your choice."

"Thanks, but I think I'd like to stay with my outfit," I said. Nearly a year passed before I returned to the States--and then only for my outfit to get ready for the invasion of Japan. We were loading our ship in San Diego when the A-bomb dropped, ending the war. I've often felt I would not have survived an invasion of the Japanese homeland.

Following the war, I went to the University of Oklahoma on the G.I Bill, and then on to law school. I ran for a seat in the

Oklahoma legislature while still in law school, and won. The legislature provided me a good education in politics that served me in good stead in later years; however, I chose not to run for a second term.

Repeal of prohibition almost ruined my career as a lawyer, especially among other lawyers. They tended to treat me as some kind of vigilante, a raider. I haven't lived it down yet. People still call me "Whiskey Joe" or "Cannonball Joe."

Not many people are aware of it, but I finished in the top ten percent of my law school class. I was a *good* lawyer. That may not seem important to everybody, but it's important to me. I want to be remembered as a lawyer, not as a damned whiskey raider.

The rest of the story is in the book.

Judge Joe Cannon (Ret.)
Oklahoma City, February 2001

1

Defending the Indigent

I got my first case when I was only four days out of law school. Judge Eugene Rice called. He asked, "Joe, what are you doing?" Rice was a federal judge in the Eastern District of Oklahoma with headquarters in Muskogee, where I lived.

"I'm not doing anything, Judge. I'm just sitting here. I haven't got a client yet."

"You do now," Rice said. "I've got a term of court starting on Monday, and I've got about ten cases that are indigent, and no lawyers. I'm appointing you to represent all of them."

"What?" I wasn't sure I heard him correctly.

"I'm appointing you to represent all of them."

I had always been taught that when a federal judge tells you, as a lawyer, what you're going to do, you do it. So I said, "Yes sir, Judge. I'll be there."

My situation was a little out of the ordinary. I was already a lawyer before graduating from law school. Most people took six months to a year after graduation to pass the bar. In my case, the oddity can be traced indirectly to the outbreak of the Korean War and the nation's shortage of experienced combat personnel. Having served nearly four years in the U.S. Marine Corps in the Pacific during World War II, I had every reason to believe I would be called up, whisked out to California, and then shipped off to Korea. If that happened, and assuming I spent two or three years over there, I would be at a helluva disadvantage for taking the bar when I came back after that long a hiatus.

Three other guys were in a similar fix. Accordingly, we went to

the Oklahoma Supreme Court and asked to see Chief Justice Earl
Welch. We explained to him that we were graduating seniors,
World War II vets subject to call-up, and needed to take the bar
exam while the knowledge was still fresh on our minds. Welch set
up a deal whereby we could take the bar examination early. All
four of us passed and were sworn in as lawyers while we were
still in law school.

Lemon-Spotted Coon Dog

The first case Judge Rice handed me involved a farmer arrested
in a raid on a moonshine still. The trial was set for Monday. I had
less than a week to prepare.

The defendant told me that he didn't have anything to do with
that still. He merely happened to be out there looking for his
lemon-spotted coon dog, and when the federal officers came up
they thought he was working there so they arrested him.

My first reaction was to say to myself, *Oh sure, how many
times have the feds heard that story before?* However, there was
something in this guy's answer that perked my ears.

"What kind of a dog did you say it was?" I asked.

He said, "A lemon-spotted coon dog."

Now, I had never heard of a lemon-spotted coon dog, but I
decided right then and there that was going to be my defense. I
was going to try this case on a lemon-spotted coon dog.

I put the farmer on the stand. He testified that he was out there
looking for his dog, and he didn't have anything to do with the
running of the still. He said he lived close by.

Q: What kind of a dog was it?

A: A lemon-spotted coon dog.

Q: A what?

A: A lemon-spotted coon dog.

That became my closing argument to the jury. I told them, "If
your dog was loose, and the woods were nearby, you'd be out in

the woods looking for him. This gentleman was out looking, not for just a dog, he's looking for a lemon-spotted coon dog. Now, whoever heard of a lemon-spotted coon dog? I guess there is such an animal. But he couldn't have made that story up. If he had made up the story, he would have just said, 'coon dog.'"

That was my whole argument. Then I sat down.

The jury turned him loose.

Law Partner

I shared a law office with my boyhood chum, Howard Edmondson, in our hometown of Muskogee, Oklahoma. Howard graduated from Oklahoma University Law School six months ahead of me, mainly because I was a State Representative and dropped out of law school for one semester to attend to the business of the legislature.

Pickings were slim for young lawyers. The older, more experienced attorneys had business pretty well sewed up. Lacking clients, and not content merely to sit around an empty office, Howard and I often went to the afternoon movie, bought a bag of popcorn and large Coca Cola, and amused ourselves.

As luck would have it, however, when we got home those nights we might learn our wives had already made plans for us to go to the very same movie. Howard and I frequently found ourselves sitting through a movie twice in the same day. Eventually, we "fessed up" to our wives where we had been spending our afternoons.

Accordingly, with the expenses of starting a new law practice and having no regular clients, Howard and I were happy to accept any appointments the bench might send our way.

Sammy Pumpkin

Another appointment involved a man with the unlikely name of Sammy Pumpkin. Sammy was a full-blood Cherokee, a nice-looking and respectful kid in his early twenties. He was charged with murder.

Sammy had worked as a handyman for an elderly lady who

lived in a cabin on the outskirts of Tahlequah. He did things like rake the leaves, fix the fence, and perform whatever odd jobs she might ask. He worked for her for several years.

One day he went out to her place and killed her and robbed her of whatever few dollars she had. Hell, she was drawing old-age pension, and he probably didn't get more than fifty dollars. Not only did he rob and kill her, the coroner testified that he raped her dead body--not her dying body, but her dead body. (The technical term for this act is *necrophilia.*) Then he burned the house down on top of her.

I never did understand why he did that. Sammy wasn't the kind of a person to commit a crime. He didn't have any police record. From my investigation and talking to people who knew him, he'd never before done anything harmful to anybody else.

The police caught him. He gave a full and complete written confession to the Cherokee County law officials in which he detailed exactly what he did.

An attorney named June Bliss was named to be the special prosecutor in this case. Cherokee County had a brand new, young prosecutor whom they didn't think was up to the job, whereas Bliss was a seasoned veteran.

From the standpoint of mounting a defense, the situation looked pretty grim for Sammy. The prosecution had all the evidence in the world against him. I decided the only thing I could possibly do was to try to keep them from giving him the death penalty. There was no doubt a jury would find him guilty of murder, robbery, arson, and rape--after all, he'd already confessed. The only thing I could do was mitigate the punishment.

We fought it out for over a week in the old Cherokee County courthouse in Tahlequah.

At the end, I gave what I consider to be the best closing argument to the jury that I ever made in my life. I don't want to sound braggadocio, but as Dallas quarterback and Hall of Famer, Don Meredith, once said, "If it's true, it's not bragging."

I talked about this old courthouse we were in, and if these walls could talk. I talked about Sequoyah's cabin. I talked about the tradition of when a Cherokee man was convicted of murder, and if he had crops to get in for his family, they would let him go home and get the crops in; and on the day he was supposed to come back, he'd come back that very day. And they'd hang him right there on the courthouse lawn.

It was absolutely and totally an emotional type of closing argument. Of course, I didn't have anything else to talk about. I had no facts. They had a written confession that they read to the jury. He signed it. He told them everything he did.

My statement really had nothing to do with the facts of the case. I didn't have any facts, not a single one, that I could present to the jury as to why they shouldn't kill this man.

Sammy was found guilty and sentenced to life imprisonment. But my strategy worked. He was spared the death penalty.

Sadly, that is not the end of the story. A few months later Sammy Pumpkin escaped from the prison at McAlester and killed again. He did the same thing to another woman. He robbed her, raped her dead body, and burned the house down.

That is the only murder case in over 50 years of practicing law that I still have bad feelings about. If Pumpkin had been given the death penalty, he would have been in a more secure part of the prison, namely, death row, from which he would not likely have escaped.

Ben "The Bomb" Trantham

Ben Trantham was a young man in Muskogee. He was a big husky fellow, in his mid twenties, and his whole ambition in life was to become an outlaw. He hung out around York Street, which was the tough part of Muskogee. It was home to the town's bootlegger joints and sleazy night clubs.

He trailed around with the bad guys, he talked tough like they talked, and he even tried to act tough like they acted. Nevertheless, I think they took advantage of Ben, knowing full well that he wasn't the sharpest tool in the shed.

These bad guys on York Street gave Ben his big chance. They hired him to blow up a new night club that had been built south of Muskogee. They viewed it as competition. It was a lot nicer than the smelly, run-down establishments they were running.

Ben went to an all-night filling station near the club and bought a five-gallon can of gasoline, which he charged to his own name and signed the ticket. The night club was closed and padlocked when he got there. He broke the padlock and pried open the back door to gain entry. Once inside, he poured the entire five gallons of gasoline all over the floors, furniture, and fixtures.

Then he went back out to his car to put the can away and pick up a box of matches. That activity took several minutes.

By the time Ben got back to the night club, the interior had filled with gasoline fumes. Ben probably was not aware that gasoline fumes are more dangerous than the liquid itself. An open container of gasoline will burn harmlessly, whereas a closed compartment filled with gasoline fumes will explode catastrophically.

Ben stood in the doorway as he lit a match and tossed it into the room. When he threw that match in there, it caused the damnedest explosion you ever saw. It blew that building all to smithereens. The force of the explosion sent Ben tumbling head over heels and blew him nearly 50 yards out into an adjacent empty lot. Miraculously, he wasn't killed. However, he did suffer severe burns from the searing flames.

Following that episode, Ben got a new nickname. He became famous in local circles as "Ben the Bomb."

The police caught him, of course. Ben asked me to defend him. I told him I would. After reviewing all the evidence, I told him, "Ben, you need to get a new occupation. You aren't smart enough to be an outlaw."

Ben recovered from his burns in the penitentiary hospital. I felt so sorry for him I didn't even charge him a fee.

Gay Bank Robbers

Federal Judge Royce Savage appointed me to represent a man in federal court in Tulsa. This was a big, burly ex-convict with arms like tree trunks, a bullet head, and a scowl as mean and tough-looking as any I've ever seen.

He was accused of bank robbery. The prosecution had an uncommon witness lined up to testify against him, namely, the guy's accomplice in the robbery.

This second guy was diminutive and effeminate. It seems these two guys had previously been in federal prison together where they were cellmates and lovers. The wimpy guy agreed to testify in exchange for their being sent to the same prison so they could continue to be together.

The facts of the case were that the burly guy drove the car; he handed the gun to the wimp and told him to go into the bank and rob it. The wimp did it. He came out with a huge sum of money. And off they went.

They bought a brand new Cadillac and drove clear out to Las Vegas and California. They really lived it up. By the time the FBI tracked them down and made an arrest, they had spent all the money. There wasn't enough left to pay me a respectable lawyer's fee.

I told them I'd do everything I could to help them if they would give me the Cadillac in exchange for my fee. They readily agreed. Obviously, where they were going they would have no use for a car. So they gave me the keys to the car and signed the title over to me.

I went directly to the FBI office where Charlie Sizemore and Bob French were the two special agents for the Muskogee area. I laid the title and keys down on the desk. "This is from that Tulsa bank robbery case I'm going to defend," I said. "These guys, after they robbed the bank, bought this brand-new Cadillac."

Charlie and Bob looked puzzled.

I continued, "I'm going to come back in a month after this trial is over. If you can prove they bought that Cadillac with any of the bank robbery money, then the FBI has acquired themselves a brand-new Cadillac. But if you can't prove it, then the Cadillac belongs to me."

The basis for my defense of the tough guy was that the wimp

needed him to be in the same prison because he needed his
protector. In other words, the wimpy guy would be forced into
being a penitentiary whore unless he had some big guy to protect
him. With his buddy there, he would be safe.

That was our defense, namely, that the guy was lying because
he wanted the big guy to go back to prison with him.

The wimp was headed for prison, there was no doubt about it.
They had pictures of him with a gun on the bank's security
camera.

When the wimp took the witness chair, I asked him a series of
questions about their being in prison together, how they remained
buddies when they got out, whether the big guy was his
sweetheart and protector while they were in prison, and so forth.

I turned around as if to start back to the counsel table, then I
said, "Judge, one more question."

The judge nodded OK.

I asked, "Are you in love with this big tough guy?"

The U.S. Attorney objected and just raised hell. "That's totally
irrelevant!"

Old Judge Savage sat there and thought a minute. He said,
"You're going to be overruled, because I'd kinda like to hear the
answer to that myself."

The answer was yes, he was in love with him.

My client lost, and the wimp got his wish. He ended up back in
prison with his sweetheart.

I went back to the FBI office as promised. Sizemore and French
had no proof that any of the bank's money was used to buy the
car. Accordingly, I was soon seen driving around town in a brand
new Cadillac.

Chester Lee Gonzalis

Race relations between Indians and Whites were at a low ebb in
our area, due in part, I think, to a case of frontier justice
administered by Judge Sam Sullivan.

An Indian boy was accused of raping a white girl. Judge
Sullivan organized and led a posse to capture him. The judge

refused to appoint a defense attorney for the boy but instead entered a "not guilty" plea himself. Sullivan waived the defendant's preliminary hearing and held him for trial, tried him for rape, found him guilty, and sentenced him to death--all without benefit of lawyer or jury.

Naturally, the Court of Criminal Appeals reversed Sullivan and gave him a severe tongue lashing, but the damage was already done. Indians grew distrustful of receiving justice in the white man's court.

Accordingly, I was a bit apprehensive when District Judge E. A. Summers called me to represent Chester Lee Gonzalis. This would be my first big case.

Chester Lee Gonzalis was a full-blood Cherokee Indian. He was accused of the shotgun slaying of popular Adair County sheriff Henry Buckner on a country road near Stilwell, Oklahoma. The trial was moved to Muskogee on a change of venue since he argued he couldn't obtain a fair trial in his home county.

Summers was the senior district judge in Oklahoma at the time. He lived on a farm near Wagoner, the next town north. Muskogee was one of the counties under his jurisdiction. Summers was a brilliant lawyer, famed for his knowledge of constitutional law in Oklahoma. He refused to wear a robe in court. He wore battered, high-top work boots that often had cow manure on them, and he'd often put his feet up on the desk and lean back in his chair.

One time, the supreme court told him they wanted him to come over to Oklahoma City and try a case. "You'll have to wear a robe," they said. He replied, in so many words, "Go to hell. I ain't wearing no robe." Summers had enough stature that he could get away with it.

I saw him at a trial in Sallisaw one scorching hot, summer day. Summers was sitting on the bench with no robe, wearing those cowboy boots, and clad in a tank-top undershirt. The courtroom lacked air conditioning, so he simply peeled off his shirt in order to be more comfortable. Despite these idiosyncrasies, everyone respected his ability as a judge. He was truly one of a kind.

When Summers called me to take this case, the name of the

defendant fooled me. Gonzalis is a Spanish surname. I subsequently learned that a lot of Cherokees have Spanish surnames,
many dating back to the days when Spain held sway over much of
the Cherokee lands.

I went over to Stilwell to start my investigation. I told Chester
Lee that I was there to help him. He would not talk to me at all. It
did not seem to matter that I was his attorney.

I walked around Stilwell talking to his neighbors and friends
and other people who knew him. No one would open up to me
about the case. I'd knock on doors and try to explain to them what
I wanted, and they'd shut me out. "No speak English," they'd
say. It was frustrating to talk to people who could be a witness in
the case but who wouldn't say a word.

That's when I went back to Muskogee and got in touch with
Tom Roach. He was the official interpreter for the Federal Court
in Muskogee, Eastern District of Oklahoma. A full-blood
Cherokee, Tom was about 65 years old, and trusted by both
Indians and Whites. I told him what my problem was and asked
him if he'd help me. He said he would.

Roach explained that Indian people, if you don't know them,
don't want to talk about anything important except in their native
language. They don't want to speak English, even if they can.
They want to talk in Cherokee, Sioux, Choctaw, Fox, or whatever.

He went over to Stilwell with me. We went to the same
identical people. This time they talked to Tom Roach like crazy. It
was as if a dam had burst. I got all the information I needed to
line up witnesses.

I learned that the sheriff had been dating Chester Lee's teen-age
sister and got her pregnant. He was a married man who had been
playing around on the side. The girl confirmed that the sheriff had
been her only lover and was the father of her unborn child.
Moreover, he threatened to kill Chester Lee if he told anyone
about it.

The picture that emerged was one of Chester Lee being a nice,
young kid who was trying to protect his sister.

The trial was held with the aid of an interpreter. All the Indian witnesses testified in Cherokee.

It was really an eye-opening--and often amusing--experience. For example, I might ask, "Did you go hunting that morning?"

Instead of a simple "Yes" or "No," the witness might take five minutes to answer. I'd turn to the interpreter, "What did he say?"

"He said, 'Yes.'"

Everybody would laugh--the judge, the jury, the spectators, even the prosecuting attorneys.

I said, "Tom, he's got to have said more than that. The man talked for five minutes."

Roach replied, "Well, you don't understand Cherokee people. When you ask them a question, they tell you the whole story. His answer, if you want it exactly, went as follows: He said he woke up that morning about six o'clock, and he told what the weather was, and he thought about going hunting, what gun he was going to take, and then he found some shells, and he did this and that and so forth, and finally he said he went squirrel hunting."

That was the way the Cherokee witnesses answered every question.

A key factor in shaping Gonzalis' defense was Chester Lee's claim that the sheriff shot at him first. He testified that he merely pointed his gun in the general direction of the sheriff when he pulled the trigger. He was trying to keep the sheriff from shooting again. We found an empty shell casing on the ground where the sheriff was standing. We determined by footprints exactly where Chester Lee was standing. The two men were a hundred yards apart.

Chester Lee was shooting a twelve-gauge shotgun loaded with double-ought buckshot. There's only eight pellets in a load, each slightly smaller than a .22 caliber rifle bullet.

The deputy sheriffs all testified that the sheriff always carried his revolver on an empty chamber, so in case it should fall and hit the hammer it wouldn't go off. I knew that was a bunch of bull. I'd spent almost four years in the Marine Corps, so I knew a little something about guns. I knew the deputies' claim couldn't be true, and you could hit it with a sledge hammer and it wouldn't go off because it has safety shield. Until you pull the trigger, the safety shield doesn't pull out of the way to allow the hammer to strike the bullet.

Vernie Smith was a locksmith and a qualified gunsmith in Muskogee. I subpoenaed him as a witness. He told the jury about the safety lock on that gun.

Then I called Mr. Caldwell, who was the Oklahoma representative for Smith & Wesson. I qualified him as an expert about shotguns and shells. He testified that it was a pure accident that at 100 yards one of those pellets from Gonzalis' shotgun hit the sheriff. He said you could stand there and shoot at him a hundred times and never kill a man with a shotgun. But this one pellet hit him right in the heart and killed him.

The prosecution was asking for murder one with the death penalty. When the jury came in, they found Gonzalis guilty of manslaughter in the second degree and gave him four years. Really, what they did was find him guilty of reckless conduct by shooting at the sheriff.

I was pleased with the verdict.

§ § §

2

Assisting the Prosecutor

It soon became apparent that I was not going to make a respectable living by toiling away on indigent cases in a fledgling law partnership. It was Ed Edmondson, Howard's older brother and district attorney of Muskogee County, who rescued me. He offered me a position as assistant district attorney. (Editor's note: For consistency we use the contemporary title of "district attorney" for the office formerly known as "county attorney.")

Ed Edmondson was a remarkable person, a man whom everybody judged to be a rising political star. He was a former FBI agent, World War II naval officer, second-term district attorney in Muskogee County, and was making noises about running for Congress in 1952. At age 32, Ed was six years older than Howard and me, tall, slender, auburn haired, and renowned for his public speaking ability. Indeed, he won the national oratory contest while in college.

I asked Ed one time, "Why didn't you stay with the FBI?"

"Because I knew I wanted to run for public office when I got back home," he replied, "and I knew if I wasn't a veteran I'd have two strikes against me."

Kitchen in the Courtroom

The sheriff called me one night to say there had been a murder in the little town of Warner, seventeen miles south of Muskogee.

The body was still at the murder scene when I got there, lying in a pool of blood on the kitchen floor. I had given instructions to the deputies that they weren't to move the body, inasmuch as I wanted to view the scene myself. That would help me in trying the case.

The other guy was also on the premises; he had been detained for questioning but was not yet arrested. He was an old codger, as also was the deceased.

He was also the owner of the house in which the murder occurred. It was a shabby, run-down, weather-beaten frame house in the poor section of town. I wouldn't have given a thousand dollars for it. The murder took place in the kitchen.

The deputies and I sat down and talked with the culprit at length. According to him, the two men had been friends for many years. They had dinner together earlier that evening and were playing cards at the kitchen table when an argument ensued. Apparently, like Walter Matthau and Jack Lemmon in the movies, these two spent a lot of time bickering at each other. Only this time it went too far. He said his friend attacked him, and he had to shoot the guy in self defense.

In viewing the scene, I just couldn't figure out how the shooting could have happened the way he said it did. Where the kitchen table and appliances were situated in the room did not fit with the story he told. Neither did the angle at which the bullet entered the dead man's body--that convinced me, in my own mind, that the accused couldn't have been where he said he was. Powder burns were another example: If the victim had been as close to the accused as the accused said he was, there would have been powder burns on the dead man.

The question in my mind was, how could we prove this in court? We needed to show the layout of the kitchen, where he said he was, where the other guy was coming to attack him, how he was coming, etc. The other guy couldn't have come straight at him, as the accused claimed, because the table was between them.

The closer we got to the trial date, the more concerned I became that charts and diagrams alone wouldn't be enough to explain all that to the jury. We had a written statement from the guy that would be hard to disprove. I thought the jury needed to see the death scene. But it was impractical to transport the jury to the murder scene, so I decided to transport the murder scene to the jury.

I called a friend of mine who bore the nickname "Hog" Malone. Hog and I were political enemies but personal friends. Nearly every day we ate lunch at the same little cafe. He acquired his nickname from the prodigious amounts of food he was able to put away. It was said that he could eat a dozen hamburgers, four entrees, and then the New York Times, Sunday edition, for dessert.

I asked Hog to bring his truck down to the murder site. We loaded up all the stuff from the accused's kitchen--the table, refrigerator, stove, everything that was in there. We even pulled up the linoleum from the floor.

We hauled the entire kitchen up to Muskogee and set it up in the courtroom. In order to fit it all in, we moved the counsel tables back; we laid the linoleum on the floor where the counsel tables had been; we set up all of the kitchen appliances; and we even unscrewed the bar--the railing that separates the lawyers from the spectators--and shoved it back against the first row of spectator seats. When we finished, we had an exact replica of the kitchen as it was when the killing happened.

We did the work at night, not finishing until after two in the morning.

Hog and I could have gotten into serious trouble--especially me. For many judges, their courtroom is like a church, a sanctuary, a holy place. I hadn't asked the trial judge, E.G. Carroll, for permission to invade his courtroom with all that stuff. I was afraid if I asked him in advance he would say no. I didn't ask Ed Edmondson either, for the same reason.

Carroll was a heavy-set, jolly-looking, good-old-boy type of judge in his early sixties. He had a reputation for "counting the votes" in cases he tried, namely, how many spectators are there in support of the prosecution and how many for the defendant. He was a good politician. He served in a small county where everybody knew him. However, a lot of lawyers thought his elevator didn't make it all the way to the top floor, as far as his legal knowledge was concerned.

Judge Carroll came out of his chambers the next morning to start his trial. I sat with bated breath. He looked startled. "Where did all this junk come from? And who said you could put it in my courtroom?" I stood up and said, "I did, Your Honor. I apologize. I didn't want to wake you up at two or three o'clock in the morning to ask for your permission. I needed this as an exhibit. I want it to go into the record that the courtroom as it's shown to the jury is the state's exhibit. I need it to prove that the murder didn't happen the way the confession says it happened."

"Okay," he said grudgingly. I breathed a sigh of relief. The judge sat there with a scowl on his face. It was apparent he wasn't happy about what we did, but he permitted the trial to proceed anyway.

All our work and creative effort was all for naught, however. We lost the case.

Arkansas Extradition

We ran up against a brick wall in trying to extradite a guy from Arkansas. The guy had killed a Muskogee policeman. He then hightailed it to Arkansas where he was outside the jurisdiction of the Oklahoma courts. We were trying to get him back to stand trial.

Our "brick wall" was Governor Francis Cherry of Arkansas. He refused to sign the extradition papers. The fact that Cherry was kin to our suspect's lawyer may have had some influence on the governor's decision. On the other hand, a governor doesn't have to extradite anybody. That decision is entirely up to him. He can say yes or no without giving a reason. In any event, we were frustrated by his refusal to approve the extradition.

To make matters worse, the culprit's lawyer put him in a mental hospital in Fort Smith. The guy wasn't crazy. This was just a ploy to keep him away from us.

Ed Edmondson and I cooked up a scheme to get him back. It involved the cooperation of Dick Bradley, known around town as "Digger O'Dell" after the popular character on the *Fibber McGee and Molly* radio show. Like the fictional Digger O'Dell, Bradley ran a funeral home.

We got one of Bradley's drivers to drive a hearse over to Fort Smith. There, we kidnapped the guy out of the mental hospital.

We threw him into the hearse and told the driver to take off with sirens and red lights flashing, and to get back across the border into Oklahoma as quickly as possible. "And if you are able to make it into Oklahoma," I said, "we'll be right behind you, and we can handle it from there."

What we did was not illegal. If you're in front of a judge, it doesn't make any difference how you got there. The judge is in charge. The defense can't even bring that out in front of a jury.

The U.S. Supreme Court has ruled that it doesn't make any difference how you get there. If you're in front of the judge personally, he's got jurisdiction over you. It's immaterial whether you came on your own, by extradition, or by kidnapping.

The guy's lawyer tried to bring out the fact that we had kidnapped him, but he couldn't because we objected and the judge sustained our objection.

The killer tried to act like he was insane, but it didn't work. He was found guilty and sentenced to life imprisonment.

Campaigning for Ed

In 1952, Ed Edmondson entered the race for Congress. Howard and I worked in his campaign. Being a former state legislator myself, I had a good idea of what campaigning was all about.

We toured the 16 counties in his district. We might be gone for a week at a time, making speeches and putting up signs on telephone poles, bridges, and everywhere we could find to put an Edmondson sign. Whenever we found a crowd gathered together, say, in Pryor, we'd stop and make a speech. As far as we were concerned, ten was a crowd. We had a lot of fun, but we worked at it day and night.

We got back to Muskogee after one such trip and went by Howard's house. As we walked in, we saw the dining room table set with candles, their good silverware, and fine china. Howard exclaimed, "Oh my God, this is my anniversary!"

I took one look at the situation, turned around, and left. "I'll see you later, Howard," I said over my shoulder. I didn't want to know what Jeanette was going to do.

Ed won the election and went off to Washington. I went back into private practice.

One day in early 1953, Howard came to me and said he was tired of being Ed Edmondson's little brother. He wanted some recognition, to be his own man. "As long as I stay in Muskogee," he said, "I'll always be Ed Edmondson's little brother."

I asked him what he had in mind.

"I'm going to go over to Tulsa," he said. "They've got a new district attorney over there named Bob Wheeler. I'm going to go ask him for a job as an assistant DA."

I asked, "Do you know Bob Wheeler?"

He said, "Nope. Never saw him. Never met him in my life."

"Then why in the hell do you think he's going to hire you, when he's got people over there who helped him get elected? What makes you think he's going to hire a perfect stranger from Muskogee?" I said. "You're wasting your time. He won't do that."

That evening, Howard came by my house after he'd been to Tulsa.

"How did you make out?" I asked.

"Well, he hired me."

So much for my prediction.

Howard went on to become Wheeler's chief criminal prosecutor. When Wheeler ran for another office in 1954, Edmondson ran to succeed him as district attorney. He won.

§ § §

3

Waging War on Crime

I practically grew up in the Edmondson household. My father ran off when I was only a few weeks old. I neither saw nor heard of him since. My grandmother took us in. We lived in her house while Mother made $13 a week as a clerk at Calhoun's Drygoods Store in downtown Muskogee. I really didn't have a family.

So I spent most of my time at Howard's house. He had an intact family--two parents, an older brother, Ed, and two sisters. I became a kind of adopted Edmondson. Old E.A., Howard's father, had a nickname for me; he called me "Lounge Lizard" because I was always lying around the house.

As a matter of fact, I can hardly remember a time when I wasn't a part of the Edmondson family. Whatever they did, I did. Wherever they went, I went.

The Edmondson household always echoed with lively discussions of politics. Old E.A. had been an assistant bank examiner in the administration of Governor Haskell, a Muskogee County commissioner, and an active supporter of local and state candidates. There seemed little doubt but that both boys would enter the political game.

It was not surprising, therefore, that their passion for politics should rub off on me.

Encouraged by Howard's success in Tulsa, I decided to get back into politics myself. Muskogee County had a weak district attorney in Louis Smith. I figured I could beat him, and I did. My strongest competition came from John Luton, a well-known local

attorney, who also filed for that office. He gave me a run for the
money. Smith came in third.

Since the Republicans did not put forth a candidate in 1956,
winning the run-off meant I won the general election as well.

Charlie Hammers

For some time prior to that, a bunch of us lawyers regularly ate
lunch at a restaurant named Pete Smith's in downtown Muskogee,
not far from the courthouse. A table was reserved for attorneys.
We'd all meet down there and, as might be expected, our
conversation often turned to what was going on in and around the
courthouse.

One of the most persistent rumors centered on outgoing District
Attorney Louis Smith and State Representative Charlie Hammers.
It was obvious to courthouse lawyers that Smith had been
dismissing a flurry of cases in the wake of his defeat. The word
on the street was, if you wanted to get a case dismissed you
should go to Charlie Hammers and make a deal.

Even before I took office in January, I decided to look into
these rumors and see if there was any truth to them. My
preliminary investigation led me to believe there was indeed
substantial misconduct in the DA's office.

Probably the most outlandish event occurred two days before
Smith left office. It involved the murder-kidnap of a young
divinity student. The young man was driving down a street in
Tulsa, and out of the goodness of his heart he gave a ride in his
car to a hitchhiker named Pete Williams. Williams forced the
student to drive to Muskogee, where he killed him. Thus Williams
had committed both murder and kidnap.

Louis Smith allowed him to plead guilty to murder and be
sentenced to life imprisonment. Smith did not file a kidnap
charge. On the other hand, if he had done so and Williams faced a
jury on both charges, he probably would have gotten the chair.

The whole thing smelled to high heaven. It provoked a lot of
public outcry. People were convinced that someone paid Smith to
get him to reduce Williams' sentence to life imprisonment.

Enter Howard Edmondson. As DA of Tulsa County where the kidnap took place, he asserted his authority to try Williams on the kidnap charge. Kidnapping was, at that time, one of four crimes for which the death penalty was authorized by state law--the others being murder in the first degree, aggravated rape, and armed robbery. Williams pled guilty to kidnapping. In a highly publicized penalty trial, Howard argued that Williams should receive the death penalty. The court agreed, and Williams was sentenced to die. That trial generated Howard a lot of publicity.

Based on what I already knew, I immediately launched a formal investigation when I took office. Investigators were sent out to find out what they could about whose cases were being dismissed, and why.

The key that unlocked the sorry mess fell into our laps when a man and his wife, Hubert and Elsie Ragsdale, came in to talk with me. Perhaps they heard about the investigation and were scared they might face charges. Perhaps they merely acted out of guilty consciences...who can say?

In any event, it seems that Hubert was driving his car while drunk; he had a wreck with another car on the Shawnee Bypass just north of town; and the wreck killed a person in the other car. Hubert ended up in the hospital.

Elsie Ragsdale said she went down to the DA's office to talk with Louis Smith about her husband's case. Smith told her he planned to file either a first or second degree manslaughter charge, he hadn't decided yet.

Shortly thereafter, Charles Hammer got in touch with her and said he could get her husband's manslaughter charge reduced to reckless driving. She said Hammers said he would go talk with the district attorney, Louis Smith.

She further stated that Hammers got back in touch with her and told her he had talked with Smith, and Smith said he could reduce the charge to reckless driving but it would cost her some money. When she asked how much, Hammers said it would cost $500.

Mrs. Ragsdale went on to say she told Hammers she didn't have that kind of money but she could borrow it. She went to her

Commercial Credit Corp. and mortgaged her furniture for as much
as they would allow, which was $400. The date of the loan
application was December 26, 1956. She made a withdrawal from
her savings account for the other $100.

Mrs. Ragsdale said she met Hammers at the stockyards on
December 28 and gave him the money. On December 31, Smith
filed a charge of second degree manslaughter in city court "with
the intent to reduce said charge at a later date."

That "later date" came on January 2, 1957. Elsie Ragsdale
went to Louis Smith's office; they went before a judge and, sure
enough, Smith reduced the charge to reckless driving with a fine
of $200.

What really ticked me off was the perversion of justice. There's
a helluva difference between manslaughter and reckless driving.
Reckless driving is just a misdemeanor subject to a small fine,
whereas manslaughter two is a felony punishable by up to four
years in a penitentiary. (Manslaughter one goes clear to life
imprisonment.) So here we have a man guilty of driving drunk,
killing another human being, and he gets off with just a small
fine.

We took the matter to the grand jury. After hearing testimony
from the Ragsdales and four other witnesses, the panel returned
indictments on March 19, 1957, against Louis Smith and Charles
O. Hammers. They were charged with "conspiracy to commit
offenses against the State of Oklahoma."

The trial of Charles Hammers came first. The case made quite a
stir in eastern Oklahoma. After all, the defendant was a sitting
state legislator and a person of stature in the community. Trial
was set for the court of Judge Clyde M. Followell.

It didn't take long for me to present the case for the
prosecution. Each of the witnesses testified to what they had told
us previously. Elsie Ragsdale testified about giving the money to
Charles Hammers on December 28, 1956.

Q: What did you do and where did you go--in connection
with this case?

A: I went to Commercial Credit and made application for a

loan. And - a loan on the furniture. I got my application and took it out to the hospital and had my husband sign it. I borrowed $400.00 there, and they gave me a check, and it was past banking hours, and I took it to Sears and had it cashed, and I met Charlie at five o'clock that evening and gave him $500.00.

Q: Where did you meet Mr. Hammers, that evening.

A: At the stockyards.

We brought in the loan officer from Commercial Credit Corp., who testified about the $400 loan. An officer from the savings and loan testified about Mrs. Ragsdale's savings withdrawal. All of these transactions, their amounts and dates, matched with the witnesses' stories.

At the conclusion of this testimony, I said, "The State rests."

It was now late afternoon. "Court is adjourned until 9:00 a.m. tomorrow morning," intoned Judge Followell.

My mind was not at peace. Hammers' attorney was Fred Green from Sallisaw. Green was an outstanding trial attorney, one of the best I have ever known. We fondly referred to him as the "Ole Gray Fox" because of his cunning mind and flowing white hair. I racked my brain trying to figure out what Green's defense would be.

Sure enough, when Green got up to put on Hammers' defense, he threw me a curve ball. In his opening statement he told the jury that Charlie Hammers' defense would be one of alibi. He said that on the day in question, Charlie and his nephew were on Fort Gibson Lake, down by the Fort Gibson Dam, fishing for catfish.

Then he called Charlie Hammers to the stand. Hammers made a good witness for himself. He testified that they had the boat down next to the dam, fishing, when it started to rain. He said it rained for hours and they had to bail the boat many times to keep it from sinking. He said he certainly remembered that day because it was such a harrowing experience. He acted as if they nearly died from the rainwater in the boat.

Charlie's nephew was equally convincing. He was a freckle-faced, red-haired, nice-looking boy of fourteen. His testimony corroborated Charlie's story down to the last detail. I cross-examined at length, but I was not able to shake his story at all.

Judge Followell asked me if I had any rebuttal evidence. I didn't, really, but I told the judge, "I do. However, it is getting late and the court might want to recess."

The judge announced adjournment until 9:00 a.m. the next morning. Hopefully by then I would have figured out something.

I went home to my wife and daughter. All evening long I pondered the situation. I knew in my heart that the alibi was a lie. But how could I break it? Finally, I went to bed, still searching for a solution.

At one a.m., I awoke with a start. I sat straight up in bed. The answer had come to me--the RAIN.

The rainstorm was the heart of Hammers' alibi, it was what made the alibi so believable.

But suppose it hadn't rained that day? I asked myself. Then Hammer's alibi--and his entire defense--would be flushed down the drain.

I woke up Bill Wiley, my investigator, and told him to come by and pick me up at my home. While waiting for Wiley to arrive, I looked up the home address of L.E. Worley, the official meteorologist for Muskogee.

We drove over to Worley's house. He didn't seem thrilled at being rousted out of a warm bed at two o'clock in the morning; nonetheless, he was graciously cooperative. I explained how important it was for me to know what the weather was on the day of December 28. He got out his records for the day in question. The records showed that nary a drop of rain had fallen that day.

I thanked him and told him we would be calling him as a rebuttal witness the next day, and for him to bring his records.

Next, Wiley and I drove out to Fort Gibson Dam, about ten miles away. I called in advance to have their meteorologist, Richard Chestnutt (not his real name), meet us at the Corps of Engineers' office. He was also the official weather man for the U.S. Government at Fort Gibson.

Mr. Chestnutt cordially went into the storeroom and pulled his records for December 1956. As I suspected, the records did not show any rain for December 28. I thanked him profusely and told him we'd be calling him as a rebuttal witness.

Trial resumed the next morning. Judge Followell announced, "The State may call its first rebuttal witness."

I called Mr. Worley. I had him state his name and address to the jury. He lived in Muskogee. I asked him his occupation. He said he was the official meteorologist for the Muskogee area. I asked him if he had the equipment to measure the weather and weather conditions such as rain? He testified that he did. I asked him if he kept official records of each day's weather in any kind of log? He said he had done so for more than 20 years. I asked him if he could tell the judge and jury if it had rained on a given day in the past. He said he could.

I had him get out his records. Could he tell the court what the weather was on December 28, 1956? He said yes.

Q: Did it rain on that date?

A: No.

Q: If a small cloud came over, as they sometimes do, could it have dropped a few raindrops?

A: That happens once in a while.

Q: Did it happen on December 28, 1956?

A: No.

Q: Are you positive?

A: Yes.

Q: Would your records show if it happened?

A: They would.

Q: Do your records show a trace of rain on that day?

A: They do not.

Fred Green got up to begin his cross examination. The Ole Gray Fox appeared poised for the kill. Intuitively, I knew what he was going to say; he was too good a lawyer to attack the official records.

As I anticipated, Green asked, "If it didn't rain in Muskogee on the 28th day of December, 1956, could it have rained at Fort Gibson Dam on that date?"

Worley answered, "Yes."

Q: Could it have rained *hard* at Fort Gibson Dam?

A: Yes.

Q: Has that ever happened before?

A: Yes.

Q: Why?

Worley went on to explain it was due to Fort Gibson Lake being such a large lake that it could generate its own weather.

"No further questions," Green told the court.

Fred Green turned and faced the jury with a triumphant smile. Then, as he passed my table, he grinned like the proverbial Cheshire cat and patted me patronizingly on the shoulder. He seemed confident he had cured the rain question that proved his client's alibi.

Judge Followell asked, "Any more rebuttal witnesses, Mr. District Attorney?"

"I have one more, Your Honor. The State calls Richard Chestnutt." The government meteorologist took the stand.

I asked him his name and whom he worked for. He said he was employed by the U.S. Corps of Engineers. I asked what he did for the Corps. He said he was chief meteorologist at Fort Gibson Dam.

Q: Did the State subpoena you to come to court today and bring your records?

A: Yes.

Q: Where are your office and instruments located?

A: Inside the Fort Gibson Dam.

Q: Do you have with you the official records for the 28th day of December, 1956?

A: I do.

Q: Will you tell the jury what they show?

A: There was not a drop of rain that fell that day.

Fred Green walked up to the witness chair and examined the records. This time, he didn't turn and smile at the jury. When he walked by my table, he didn't grin or pat me on the shoulder. Instead, he muttered in a voice that only I could hear, "You son-of-a-bitch.''

It felt good. I had trapped the Ole Gray Fox.

In my closing argument, I told the jury, ''Charlie Hammers was fishing that day alright...but he was fishing for bribe money and not for catfish.''

The jury found him guilty.

NOTE: Charles Hammers' conviction was subsequently reversed on grounds that the grand jury was improperly formed. Louis Smith was never tried for bribery, and his indictment was set aside by court order January 12, 1962.

State Fair

Muskogee holds a fair every year, which it calls the ''Muskogee State Fair.''

The fair's big promoter was John Lewis Stone, managing editor of the *Muskogee Phoenix*. Although the newspaper itself was owned by the Bixby family, the fair was Stone's baby.

In addition to the rides, rodeos, food courts, and other forms of amusement, there was always a large number of carnival games where people could win prizes such as Kewpie dolls, teddy bears, stuffed tigers, etc. Some of the prizes were fairly expensive.

Once in a while you'd see a kid walking around with one of those expensive prizes, but not often. The ''carnies'' who operated the games only allowed there to be a few winners in order to entice other people to play the game. It was a sucker bet all the way.

I knew they were crooked, so I resolved to clean up their act. Along with my principal investigator Bill Wiley and one of the deputy sheriffs, I paid an unannounced visit to the fair.

One of the games we visited had about a hundred strings hanging from the roof of the booth. Theoretically, some of those strings were tied to prizes. If you pulled the lucky string you would pull up one of the prizes, and it became yours to keep. I suspected there was something fishy about it.

I sent the deputy sheriff around to the back of the booth to make sure they didn't pull some shenanigan on us.

Then Wiley and I went to the front of the booth where we took each string and pulled it, one at a time until we had pulled them all. Not a single prize moved off the shelf.

We visited another booth that had a trough across the front with water in it and rubber ducks floating on top. The bottom of each duck was marked with a number. If you chose a duck with one of the winning numbers, you'd win a prize.

We followed the same routine as before. The deputy went around to the back, and Wiley and I walked up to the front of the booth. As soon as we knew the deputy was in place, I put my arm across the trough to stop the ducks from floating by. We checked every duck, and not a one had a winning number. The deputy reported that all the ducks with winning numbers were sitting on a shelf in the back. The operator had a confederate back there who once in a while would put a winner in the trough--just often enough to keep the players coming back.

I had seen enough. The carnies were cheating the people of this county, and worse, cheating these little kids. So I had the deputy to get on his radio and call in a bunch of other deputies. We arrested everyone who operated a game.

We not only arrested the people who operated the games, we also confiscated all their prizes. In my view, the prizes were part of the gambling game. And since gambling was illegal in Oklahoma, this was an illegal operation.

I took them all to jail. I told them they could take their choice. Either I could get them on a misdemeanor charge and confiscate all their prize merchandise, or they could sit here in jail, get a bondsman and a lawyer, and fight it in court under the heaviest penalty there is for operating a gaming device.

It wasn't much of a choice. They took the first option.

We loaded all the merchandise into an 18-wheeler--there must have been a thousand prizes in all--and took them to the state orphanage at Guthrie. I called the superintendent of the orphanage and told him what we were doing. I said, "Give them out to the kids at your discretion." So we took all those prizes to Guthrie and gave them out to the kids.

John Lewis Stone was absolutely incensed. He had a lot of power. He got a delegation of businessmen together--probably the paper's heavy advertisers. They came down to the courthouse to ask me to return all the merchandise and let the fair operate.

"No way," I told them.

Failing that effort, they went up to see the district judge, Andrew Wilcoxen. They asked him to issue an injunction against me. Andy pulled out the statutes and said, "Do you want to be part of the conspiracy to violate the gambling laws?"

They hemmed and hawed.

Andy said, "That's what I'd be doing if you get me to sign that order you have requested. It's a penitentiary offense. Now are you sure you want me to sign it?"

They didn't want any part of it. The crowd melted away.

(Later, one courtroom pundit suggested this wasn't really gambling because you didn't stand a chance of winning.)

Tree Trimmer

Undoubtedly, one of the weirdest cases I ran into occurred when we sought to raid a gambling house in a predominantly black neighborhood of north Muskogee. This was a large, two-story house, and every Saturday night they held a big gambling party with dozens of players in attendance.

Sheriff Bill Vinzant and I decided to raid the place. We hit the place about midnight with a large team of deputies.

When the officers crashed the front door, the players took off like a covey of quail. Some jumped out first and second-story windows, some tried to run out the back door, and others battered through sheetrock walls. In some instances, one could discern an imprint of the person who went through the wall.

Vinzant and I stationed ourselves under a big oak tree in the front yard. We saw one player jump out a second-story window, dust himself off, and start to run away. Unfortunately, his eyes were not adjusted to the dark and he ran straight into the arms of the sheriff.

The guy came to a stop and began looking up at the oak tree and walking around it. After three or four circuits I asked him, "What in the world are you doing?"

He replied, "Mr. Joe, I'm a tree trimmer and I'm figuring a job."

Vinzant and I got so tickled with a preposterous story like that we turned him loose.

The rest went to jail.

Serial Rapist

A rapist was on the loose in west Muskogee. Women living alone were being raped by what we judged to be a serial rapist. This went on for several months.

His *modus operendi* was to break in, hold a chloroform-soaked cloth over the woman's mouth until she fell unconscious, then rape her. By the time the victim awoke and could call the police, the rapist was long gone.

The police nearly caught him one time. A squad car happened to be patrolling nearby when the call came in. They broke down the door and rushed into the victim's bedroom. The rapist leapt across her bed, dived through a partially opened window, and got away.

In each of the rape cases, the woman described a similar method of operation. They also gave essentially the same physical description of their assailant. He was a black male, six feet tall, and weighed between 190 and 200 pounds.

In addition, the women were also consistent in saying he had one distinguishing characteristic, namely, a peculiar odor. They said his body exuded an odor they had never smelled before, an odor they couldn't identify.

Something had to be done. We had to put a stop to this man. The situation was getting out of hand. Husbands, fathers and brothers began sitting up all night with a gun across their knees. One man nearly shot his own son when the boy went around the house to check on a noise. Every female in the western part of town was on a high state of alert; before going to bed they pecked in their closets, looked under their beds, and locked the windows. Lacking air conditioning, sleeping became very uncomfortable behind closed and locked windows in the hot and humid summer nights.

I organized a Rape Task Force. It consisted of my two investigators, the county sheriff and deputies, and several highway patrol officers, as well as myself.

We spread out over the west side of the city. Each car was equipped with a police radio. Several times we got calls, but even though we were only a few blocks away he had already escaped by the time we could get there. With all the law enforcement officers we had covering the area, it was a mystery how he could get away without being seen.

I decided to take what information we had and see if we couldn't figure out how he was eluding our screen. The answer that came to mind was that he must be disappearing down a manhole in the street and escaping through the city's storm drain system.

Muskogee is subject to heavy downpours of rain and flash flooding. Consequently, it has a massive storm drain system. The system empties into Coody Creek, which, in turn, flows into the Arkansas River. The main drain is so large that one can drive a truck through it.

Bill Wiley, possibly one of the best investigators I ever worked with, would work night and day if I needed him. We pored over the city's maps of the sewer system and determined that we could get almost anywhere the rapes were occurring. A special tool was required to lift the manhole cover; but since the tool could be obtained from any plumbing shop, we figured our rapist would have no difficulty acquiring one.

Officers were assigned to check out the various manholes. Wiley and I went down one of them ourselves. My God, it smelled awful! We determined that it was feasible for our rapist to use the sewer system as an escape route. However, if we were expecting to see the culprit, we were due for a disappointment; the only living things we saw down there was an army of huge rats.

Another time, we got a call from a house where the rapist had been reported. We arrived ahead of the police. I told Bill to check out the detached garage in back of the house while I looked inside the house to see if he might still be there.

Nothing inside. When I stepped back outside, however, I heard the damnedest noise. Here came Bill rounding the corner of the house waving his gun. I asked him what happened. He said he damned near shot the people's cat. He said the cat scampered past him when he entered the garage, and it knocked a bunch of cans and things off the storage shelves in its effort to get away.

The Muskogee Police later told me a different version of the story. They said they arrived in time to see the cat run out of the garage all right; however, they depicted Bill as being so startled by the noise that he screamed and threw his gun up the air.

Descriptions of the rapist continued to pour in. It finally dawned on me that they resembled a person I knew who ran a photo processing business. I went down to his store to talk to him. The minute I walked through the front door I was beset by a peculiar odor. It was the film developing fluid.

I obtained a bottle of the developing fluid. Then I went around to every lady who had been raped, soaked a rag in the fluid, and asked her to smell it. Without exception, they all identified the odor as being the same as what they smelled during the crime.

We brought the guy in for questioning. I was sure we had our man. We questioned him for hours but were unable to break his story. In the end, we had to let him go because of a lack of evidence.

Even though our suspect was never prosecuted for rape, the rapes ceased. We never had another one of this kind.

I guess one could say we were successful in preventing future rapes. By coming down so hard on this guy, we apparently scared him off. Nevertheless, I would have felt better if we could have prosecuted and convicted the man who committed the rapes of all those women.

Writing the Statute

We had an infant death on our hands. A woman came in, hysterical, and told us her husband was drunk and had just beaten her baby to death.

Bill Vinzant and I drove out there in the sheriff's car. It was snowing like hell. A tiny baby was lying in its crib. We could find no signs of life. The child died of a broken skull. The murder weapon was its own bottle.

The husband was asleep. He was clad only in his underwear. Bill Vinzant jumped on top of him, handcuffed him, dragged him through the house by the chain that connected the handcuffs, bounced him down the stairs, down the front porch steps, through the snow, and threw him in the back of the sheriff's car. I had never seen Bill so mad; I was afraid he was going to kill the guy.

I had to dismiss the case against this baby-killer because I couldn't prove it. The only witness we had was his wife. And she couldn't testify against him because he was her husband.

It was a matter of law that a wife could not be forced to testify against her husband, and vice versa. She could, but she didn't have to. The privilege was his. She wanted to testify but he wouldn't give his permission.

We got a lot of public outcry over the decision not to prosecute. It made us sick that we couldn't prosecute him, but we couldn't. That's when I sat down and wrote an amendment to Statute 2504 which dealt with husband-wife privilege. My proposed amendment would modify the husband-wife privilege in such a way that when one or the other of them commits a felony against their minor child, whether the child be from their marriage or a spouse's prior marriage, one may testify against the other.

I went to see Harold Shoemake who was our state senator from Muskogee. Shoemake liked my proposed amendment and had me come to Oklahoma City to testify before the Senate Committee on Criminal Jurisprudence. I told committee members the story of what happened to the baby and why we had to turn the killer loose.

I pointed out that my proposed amendment specifically limited the crime to a "felony." Parental spanking and disciplining a child isn't a felony. We didn't want to turn the district court into a domestic relations court. "My God," I said, "We wouldn't get anything done. The court would be bogged down with all sorts of family squabbles."

The committee didn't hesitate a minute to adopt the amendment and send it to the floor of the senate. No one even argued about it. The law now reads:

2504. Husband-Wife Privilege

D. There is no privilege under this section in a proceeding in which one spouse is charged with a crime against the person or property of:

1. The other;

2. A child of either;

3. A person residing in the household of either; or

4. A third person when the crime is committed in the course of committing a crime against any other person named in this section.

§ § §

4

Electing Edmondson

I didn't get heavily involved in Howard's campaign for governor until the polls closed on primary election night on July 22, 1958. Until then, my own campaign for reelection as district attorney took all my time and attention. My challenger was none other than Louis Smith, who was trying to win his old job back. He didn't get anywhere.

The polls closed at 7:00 p.m. My wife, Caroline, and I jumped in our car and headed to Tulsa to sweat out the primary returns with Howard at his campaign headquarters.

On our way out of Muskogee, we stopped for gas. The filling station was owned by a fellow who ran for sheriff against Bill Vinzant, a very popular incumbent. Just to be sociable, I asked the man, "How is the sheriff's race going?"

"Joe, I think I've won it. Everybody I talked to today says he voted for me."

That poor, deluded soul. The final tally showed he got only eight votes. Hell, he couldn't even get his whole family to vote for him.

Eleven prominent Democrats had entered the race. Among them were Andrew Wilcoxen, district judge from Muskogee; George Miskovsky, state senator from Oklahoma City; W.C. Doenges, Tulsa automobile dealer; and W.P. "Bill" Atkinson, millionaire founder and developer of Midwest City. Atkinson was by far the most formidable opponent; he didn't need to raise campaign money--he had enough of his own.

The results of the primary surprised most Oklahomans. Very few experts had taken Howard seriously. As it turned out, he received the largest number of votes. Atkinson came in a close second. The two would face each other in a run-off election.

Primary election night also brought one of the most seductive and potentially compromising decisions that Edmondson ever had to face. Late that evening, when it became clear that Howard had built up a snug lead and was safely into the run-off, we got a call from two road contractors. One was Al Kavanaugh from Oklahoma City, and the other was Ray Smith of Tulsa. (Smith also owned the Tulsa Oilers baseball team.) They asked to meet with us. We set a meeting date for the next day.

Present at the meeting were Howard Edmondson, Congressman Ed Edmondson, Leland Gourley, and myself. Kavanaugh and Smith pointed out how expensive it was going to be to conduct a run-off campaign against Bill Atkinson. It would cost over a million dollars.

"The election is only three weeks away," they began. "You should be out campaigning instead of raising money." They offered to finance Howard's run-off campaign, no matter what it cost. They said, in effect, "You all go out and campaign and don't worry about the money. We will come up with the money."

Kavanaugh and Smith didn't ask for any *quid pro quo*. Their proposal was not illegal. There was no bribe, nor offer of a bribe. In reality, it was little different than a modern-day political action committee (PAC).

On the other hand, the natural inference was that they were seeking to gain influence with the governor's office. Such influence could come in handy when it came time to bid state highway projects. At a time when four-lane highways were costing a million dollars a mile to construct, one can readily see why they'd be interested in gaining whatever advantage they could.

Ed spoke first. "No. Absolutely not!" He answered before any of the rest of us had a chance to say anything. Howard asked around the room. Leland said no. I said no. Howard said no. Following that conversation, we set a limit of $1,000 on campaign contributions.

With the runoff set for August 12, we didn't take time for a victory party. Instead, we got right to work with a planning meeting. Howard named me to manage the eastern part of the state. Whit Pate, a lawyer from Poteau, became manager for western Oklahoma. He and his friend Jake Blevins worked their butts off. My wife agreed to help Jeanette Edmondson with correspondence, organizing ladies' teas, and so forth.

Caroline was a tall, good-looking, energetic, woman of twenty-three. She was blessed with an uncommonly strong touch of earthy horse sense. Caroline had worked as a secretary, could take shorthand, and typed like a bandit. Every letter that went out from Howard's office was typed individually.

Caroline also happened to be pregnant during the campaign. (Our son, Scott, was born the following March.) She jokingly referred to her pregnancy as an "immaculate conception." Because I was on the road so much of the time, she said, she couldn't figure out how she got in a family way.

The next three weeks were spent campaigning full time for Howard. Caroline and I moved into a suite of rooms in the Mayo Hotel that were made available to us without charge by Burch Mayo, the hotel's owner and Edmondson supporter. It was entirely Mayo's idea that we stay there. The hotel was within walking distance of the Edmondson headquarters, and it would save us an hour's drive back and forth to Muskogee every day. Leland Gourley occupied the connecting room.

I spent all day every day at Howard's Tulsa headquarters--and often until late at night. Although technically his manager for eastern Oklahoma, I really functioned as the *de facto* second in command. After all, Howard and I had grown up together, we pursued parallel career paths, and we understood how each other thought. He trusted me to represent him.

Leland Gourley saw to the printing and distribution of the

campaign's newspaper, *The Prairie Fire News*. Leland was a member of the inner circle of campaign advisors. As owner and publisher of the *Henrietta Daily Freelance,* he was the first newspaper to come out in support of Edmondson's candidacy. He wrote speeches, generated publicity, placed ads, mined his vast network of media contacts, and did whatever Howard asked

He also owned a radio station. He told the station manager, "If Cannon wants to stop and make a speech for Howard, just turn it over to him." So every time I'd be passing through the area campaigning, I'd stop and make a speech. He didn't charge us a thing. Probably it should have been reported as an in-kind campaign contribution.

In his early thirties, of average height, full head of dark hair, and studious-looking, Leland Gourley was a high-energy person and a man on the go. His brain was always bursting with new ideas, sometimes tumbling out faster than we could digest them.

Pete DeFelice, along with Leland, was in charge of *The Prairie Fire News.* Pete owned an advertising agency in Tulsa. He was our advertising agent. He's the one who usually booked our television shows.

John Kilpatrick was campaign treasurer. He handled the money and all reporting of campaign contributions.

Sam Crossland was another close advisor. He was an assistant DA in Tulsa under Howard. It was Sam who wrote the words to Howard's campaign song that everybody in the state was singing. It was based on the rollicking tune "Harrigan," and it went something like this: "H-A-double-R, I-GAN, spells Harrigan."

Our version went, "E-D-MON, D-SON, spells Edmondson." No question about it, it was a catchy tune. Every time you turned the radio on, you'd hear "E D MON D...."

Television played a big role in Howard's campaign. Lacking the name recognition of Bill Atkinson, who also enjoyed the suspport of newspaper mogul E.K. Gaylord, Howard gambled he could win by using the modern-day medium of television. No politician had ever tried it before--at least on the scale he was proposing.

Before entering the gubernatorial race, Howard's notoriety rested largely on two cases he prosecuted in Tulsa--the Pete Williams kidnap of a divinity student, and the Nanny Doss criminal case. The latter case involved a woman who killed six "lonely heart" husbands for their insurance. The case gained so much publicity that Howard was invited to speak at numerous civic clubs throughout the state. Yet his strength was still not statewide, but largely confined to Tulsa and eastern Oklahoma.

He and television seemed to be made for each other. He had a deep soothing voice, wavy red hair, strong-featured face with a Robert Mitchum dimple in his chin, and impelling visual contact. Consequently, every dime we could raise went to buy television time.

I didn't know whether he could or couldn't do it. I didn't know anything about television as a campaign tool. We'd never used the medium before. We'd always handed out hand cards, put up posters, made speeches on the back of trucks. I remember my first political speech was from the back of a pickup truck.

Youthful, vibrant, charming, and articulate, Howard came across with spellbinding power when using this new medium. We arranged to have his speeches simulcast throughout the state. If you turned on a TV when Howard was giving a speech, you got Howard. I don't care where you were--Oklahoma City, Tulsa, Lawton, Wichita Falls, even Fort Smith--we had the whole state blanketed. It took a superhuman effort by Pete DeFelice to get the stations all linked together.

Howard was a television producer's dream. He had an uncanny ability to make a televised speech without using notes or teleprompter, and to finish it exactly on time--whether it be one minute, 15 minutes, or 30 minutes in length.

Repeal of prohibition emerged as the number one issue in the campaign. The issue was framed during the primary when we had George Miskovsky in there talking about repealing prohibition, and Bill Atkinson and W.C. Doenges running on a "dry" platform. Miskovsky finished fourth in the primary and Doenges fifth. Atkinson came in a close second.

Some thought Howard was for prohibition, others thought he was for repeal. Of all of the speeches he made, and of all the literature he put out, Howard Edmondson never said he was for repeal of prohibition.

The only thing he ever said was, "We are either going to have enforced prohibition, or we're going to repeal it." That was the only thing he would ever say when reporters asked him the question. He would not give them a yes or no answer. He'd simply say, "Enforcing the laws of the state will be my number one priority. I am for the people deciding the repeal issue, and I will submit it to a vote of the people on a special election within 90 days after taking office."

Hence, the wets came to believe Howard Edmondson was their man, while the drys thought he was solidly in their camp. Meanwhile, Bill Atkinson was saddled with being identified with the dry position and eventually he came to believe it was an albatross around his neck.

Leland, Caroline, and I got kicked out of the Mayo Hotel during the campaign. We came back one night after a full day on the road and found all our stuff setting out in the hall in boxes.

Caroline had her key handy so she opened the door and went in first. Leland and I trailed behind. She saw a man lying on the bed, fully clothed. He raised up and asked, "What are you doing here? I didn't call for a woman."

The problem turned out to be a mix-up in communication between Burch Mayo and his hotel manager. The manager kicked us out for non-payment of rent, whereas Mayo intended the rent to be free.

"What is Charlie Yadon up to?" I asked. Charlie, a student at the University of Oklahoma, was calling in orders for campaign literature faster than we could fill them. One day he might ask for 300 bumper stickers, and the next day call for 300 more.

I got on the phone with him the next time he called. Charlie was a friend of ours from Muskogee, now living in Norman. On his own initiative, he organized a group of students to campaign for Edmondson.

They were nothing if not persistent. They would set up a booth on campus, say, in front of the student union building. Campus police would come along, tell them it was illegal, and run them off. Every time that happened, they merely packed up their gear, moved to a new location, set it up, and started all over again.

We wound up the run-off campaign with a big statewide rally at the Civic Center in Oklahoma City. I helped plan the event.

Howard and Jeanette rode with Caroline and me from Tulsa. I drove the car. Howard fidgeted all the way. He fretted that the turnout might be light, which could result in an embarrassing situation.

He wouldn't let me park the car when we first arrived at the Civic Center in Oklahoma City. Instead, we drove slowly around the building a time or two to see what we could see. Lots of people milling around. Howard still was not satisfied.

I double-parked and went inside to check out the crowd. Howard remained in the car. I found it almost impossible to squeeze through the front door because of the large number of people milling around the lobby. Myriads of helium-filled balloons of all colors floated overhead. People wore straw hats with red, white and blue bands that had Edmondson's name emblazoned on them. Scores of ladies were togged out in dresses of red, white and blue with Edmondson pins.

I went back to the car to tell him everything was great. He was elated.

When Howard made his entrance, the crowd went wild. The band struck up his theme song, and everyone began singing and swaying with their hands held high in the air.

We handed out small gold key lapel pins and told people they were now "key men for Edmondson." The keys went like hotcakes. The rally was a huge success.

Election day is the longest day in a politician's life. There is absolutely nothing you can do.

A bunch of us were sitting around Mike Pedrick's swimming pool in Tulsa. Mike owned Vigo Dog Food and had an Aero Commander airplane with which he flew us around the state. We were relaxing, talking, and waiting for the polls to close. Someone suggested, "Why don't we call Rabbit Poole to see how the count is going?"

Rabbit Poole was the voting inspector of Precinct 31A in north Muskogee. He was one of our boys.

I called him up and said, "Rabbit, how's the vote going down there? How many votes does Howard have?"

"Mr. Edmondson has over a hundred."

"Tell me how many votes does Mr. Atkinson have?"

"Mr. Cannon, right at the moment, he ain't got none."

I said, "Rabbit, that can't be. You just can't do that! You've got to let Mr. Atkinson have some votes...or else somebody, somewhere, is going to throw the whole precinct out."

That was Rabbit, all right. He knew how to get the votes. We could always count on him to deliver his precinct.

Howard decisively defeated Atkinson in the run-off election. Next came the general election

He was a shoo-in. Phillip Colgan Ferguson, the Republican nominee, was a weak candidate. The general election took place on November 11. When the ballots were finally tallied, Howard had won by a vote of 399,504 to 107,495, the largest majority in the state's history.

Thus, Howard Edmondson became, at age 33, the youngest governor in the nation. He was so youthful in appearance, in fact, that strangers had difficulty in believing he was a governor. His youthfulness got him an appearance on the popular national television show, "What's My Line," in which panel members tried to guess his occupation.

§ § §

5

Ending Prohibition
(By Enforcing It)

Victory was sweet. But the time to celebrate was short. Much work needed to do be done between November and January when Howard would take office. Chief among these tasks was to select capable people to fill the highest offices in the state.

Wednesday, November 12--the day after the election--found us already at work in a planning session. Howard called together his regular team of campaign leaders to meet at his mother-in-law's cabin at Fort Gibson Lake.

Some of the jobs were easy to fill. Leland Gourley, for example, was named to be Howard's chief of staff. John Kilpatrick, campaign treasurer, would go to the Oklahoma Turnpike Authority. Max Genet would head the tourism bureau. I was slated to become first legal advisor to the governor.

We labored way into the night. Sustained by copious amounts of coffee, our energy level was still high at about 1:30 in the morning when Howard suddenly said we needed to keep our promise about enforcing prohibition or repealing it. After some discussion of how best to do it, we settled on the Oklahoma Highway Patrol as the appropriate agency to handle the enforcement end of things.

Howard then said, "We need someone to head it, to be the new commissioner of public safety."

The room fell deathly silent. We looked at each other.

Howard turned to me. "Joe, there's only one person in this

room who can do it, and that is you.''

It never dawned on me that I would be the one to do the prohibition thing. I said, ''Howard, I don't want it.''

He said, ''But I want you to.''

After a long and arduous discussion, I finally said I would take the job but I needed to talk it over with my wife.

Howard and I got in the car and drove over to Muskogee. I reminded him that Caroline and I had a three-year-old daughter, Dana, and a second child on the way, as well as having to sell a house in Muskogee and buy a new one in Oklahoma City. Howard had promised an April vote on the prohibition issue. Hence, if I took this job I'd be 100 percent occupied with it for another three months.

Howard turned his charm on Caroline. He presented it to her as her patriotic duty. He asked, ''Can you handle it for ninety days?''

''I can handle anything for ninety days,'' she replied.

The Enabling Act

Oklahoma carved a niche for itself in history in 1907 when it became the only state to enter into statehood with prohibition in its constitution. Prior to statehood, the federal government had been enforcing a policy of prohibition in Indian Territory. The Oklahoma Enabling Act, passed by Congress in June 1906 required the new state to continue that policy for a period of twenty-one years. Rather than divide the state into two parts, half ''dry'' and half ''wet,'' the founding fathers instituted prohibition throughout the entire state.

Over the next fifty years, five separate attempts were made to repeal prohibition. All five attempts failed. Howard's initiative would be the sixth.

Prohibition was ''honored more in the breach than in the law.'' Liquor flowed freely to those who wanted it. Will Rogers was widely quoted as saying that Oklahomans will always vote dry as long as they can stagger to the polls.

Part of the problem lay in the fact that although bootlegging was breaking the law, the bootleggers were not stigmatized as lawbreakers. The general public just sort of winked at their offenses. Moreover, Oklahoma's borders were porous, meaning that liquor could flow freely from neighboring states. There was little to stand in the way of a private automobile entering the state with a load of contraband whiskey from Missouri, Kansas, Colorado, Texas, or Arkansas.

Organizing the OHP

Howard Edmondson was sworn into office on January 13, 1959. The first thing I did was to go over to the office of Paul Reed, the outgoing commissioner of public safety. He was packing his personal stuff, preparing to vacate the office. I picked his brain about things we could do.

My next task was to call a meeting of the "brass" of the highway patrol. Structured along lines of the military, the Oklahoma Highway Patrol (OHP) had a colonel at the top, a lieutenant colonel as second in command, majors, captains, and lieutenants. I named Ray Page to be my second in command. He had a strong background in law enforcement and came highly recommended by Mike Pedrick.

I told the officers that one of my directives was to use the highway patrol in the enforcement of prohibition. I said we needed all the troops we could get. I assured them we had the full cooperation of the Oklahoma State Bureau of Investigation (OSBI), under director Forrest Castle, and that three county sheriffs joined our effort: Bob Turner of Oklahoma County, Bill Vinzant of Muskogee County, and Dave Faulkner of Tulsa County.

Some of the brass had been in the patrol for many, many years and did not want to change. They said the highway patrol was not intended to do that kind of enforcement.

I showed them the Oklahoma statutes that said on orders from the governor, they had the authority to enforce *any* laws of the State of Oklahoma. I said I had just such an order from the governor stating that the highway patrol was to be the main body to enforce the liquor laws. I informed them that was exactly what we were going to do.

Three or four members of the high brass decided to retire. That was fine with me. It gave me a chance to promote new blood. Another major wanted to argue. I said, "You're not in command. The governor is in command, and I take my orders from him. You either take your orders from me, or you're fired."

I had to fire a few recalcitrants before everybody got the message. In all, I removed eight people from the payroll.

Those officers that remained were really "gung ho." Having cleared out the deadwood at the top, they were primed for action and ready to go. Moreover, we encountered absolutely no resistance from the patrolmen on the beat. Raids and roadblocks gave them some exciting activity to relieve the monotony of driving up and down the same stretch of highway all day every day.

There were a few things I didn't like about what the highway patrol was doing. When I took over, I changed those practices. Specifically, I communicated to each and every patrolmen that the following "dirty tricks" practices were outlawed:

1. Driving at the exact speed limit.
2. Hiding behind billboards.
3. Stopping pretty girls in sports cars.
4. Driving slow with a long line of cars behind them.
5. Quotas on the number of arrests.

I made it clear to the patrolmen that if they were caught violating these rules they'd better start looking for a different job.

Also, I reinforced the notion that their job was to serve and protect the people on the roads and highways. If they saw a lady with a flat tire, for example, they should stop and offer help.

I had read many news stories about how the western highways became impassable in major snowstorms. Drifts as high as six or eight feet might block the roads, stranding motorists for several hours or even days. So I had the highway patrol purchase several four-wheel-drive vehicles that were capable of pushing their way through such drifts. The rescue squad used these vehicles to rescue stranded people.

Often, these stranded families had little kids huddled in the back seat trying to stay warm. They would be surprised to see a black-and-white pull up alongside and offer help. Some grateful people offered to pay, but it was not the patrol's policy to accept payment.

Raids and Roadblocks

We wasted little time launching the biggest effort at law enforcement in the history of the state. It began on January 18, when a roadblock set up to catch a bank robber yielded twenty-nine cases of whiskey. Five nights later, we set up roadblocks on roads leading into Oklahoma, using twenty-eight patrolmen in fifteen cars. The following night, fifty officers blocked roads along the Missouri border and searched all cars entering the state.

Moonshine was not our primary concern. To be sure, there were many tiny, back-woods stills in operation, but in the larger scheme of things they contributed little to the overall problem. By far the largest amount of alcohol consumed was brand liquors--mostly whiskey--from legitimate dealers in other states where liquor was legal. Our raids confiscated such popular brands as Jim Beam, Jack Daniels, Seagrams, Cutty Sark, and so on.

We didn't merely target bootleggers. We also went after hotels, night clubs, and honky-tonks. I had the highway patrol compile a list of every hotel and night club that sold liquor. I sent a letter to 182 hotels and 200 clubs warning them that they would be subject to prosecution if alcohol was found on their premises. Raids began January 29.

We raided a club at Spavinaw Lake in northeastern Oklahoma that was reported to do a big business selling liquor. Our initial search turned up two hidden stashes. Based on this, we started searching in earnest. We tore open floors, ceilings and walls looking for more liquor. The club's owner was standing beside me, watching the goings-on, and giving us a lot of guff. I told him he could either stay and watch us search, or he could go to jail. He shut up.

By the time we left, the place was in shambles. However, we confiscated over a hundred cases of whiskey.

One of our favorite stunts was to have a highway patrol car park outside the front entrance of a club, and just sit there. Customers were very reluctant to go in. One club owner called me and complained, "You're ruining my business."

I said, "You stop selling whiskey, and I'll move that highway patrol car out of there."

Publicity

The news media followed me around wherever I went. I made, as they say in the trade, "good copy." And to my way of thinking, all publicity was good publicity. To encourage plenty of coverage, I often allowed members of the press to ride to raids and roadblocks in highway patrol cars.

My practice was to keep the press informed. I told them I was trying to be as open as I could in order to help them in their job of keeping the public informed.

I devised a system to make it look as if I was everywhere. It involved the creative use of the highway patrol plane. One night, for example, we had five roadblocks set up in five different locations across the state. I had the highway patrol pilot fly me to all five sites, and to make sure I was seen at each of them.

The publicity did more than the courts. Whereas the courts dismissed several cases due to defective warrants and other technicalities, the seizure of alcohol caused a great expense to bootleggers and club owners. Businesses began feeling the economic pinch. Hotels began losing convention bookings.

Lieutenant Governor George Nigh coined a new drink in my honor. He called it the "Cannon Ball Cocktail." It consisted of 3.2 beer in a champagne glass. Three-point-two beer was legal; champagne was not.

Incidentally, Nigh's bit of humor also spawned a nickname that has forever stuck with me. The newspapers began calling me

"Cannonball Joe."

Directly and indirectly, our raids and roadblocks significantly reduced the amount of alcohol available in Oklahoma. More importantly, they kept public attention focused on the issue of repeal.

LIFE Magazine

The main reason I wanted to get as much publicity as possible was because I needed to create a *myth*. A myth is something people believe to be true in order to explain what is happening. I knew I could not completely dry up Oklahoma. But I had to make people believe I could--in other words, create the myth that I could. Otherwise, as long as the wets believed they could have their liquor, nothing was going to change.

That's why I said yes when a request came from *LIFE* magazine to accompany us on one of our raids.

A report came to us about a farmhouse in northeastern Oklahoma near the Missouri border that was really a central distribution point for bootleg booze. Based on this information, I told the *LIFE* boys that we were going to raid one of the biggest bootleg places in Oklahoma.

LIFE sent a photographer and a reporter. We let them ride in a highway patrol car. Several other media hounds accompanied us on the raid.

It was late when we arrived. It was a big, two-story farmhouse set out in the middle of the countryside. The place was dark. I rang the doorbell.

An older gentleman, probably in his late sixties, came to the door, obviously just having awakened from sleep. He was wearing the long-handled underwear that he slept in. That struck me as being very strange attire for a bootlegger.

I served him the search warrant, and the officers went in and spread out through the house. They opened drawers, peered in closets, and looked in every place they thought a stock of contraband whiskey might be hidden.

Through it all, the *LIFE* photographer was busy snapping

pictures, and the reporter was writing copious notes.

But the house just wasn't the kind of place I associated with a whiskey runner. It looked like an ordinary family home. The living room was furnished with ordinary tables, ordinary chairs, ordinary cabinets, and ordinary knick-knacks on ordinary shelves. I kept thinking, *This doesn't fit. This can't be what we thought it was.*

Finally, I came to the very reluctant conclusion that we had made a terrible mistake. This man was not a bootlegger. He didn't have anything to do with running booze. He was a farmer.

The man's wife came out. Hearing the noise, she put on a robe and came out to see what we were doing to her house.

Having convinced myself we had made a helluva mistake, I told the officers to go outside, get in their cars, and wait for me. "You all wait for me out there, but get out of the house. Get out of here!"

I called all the news media together. I specifically told them that we made a mistake. "This man is not a bootlegger. He has nothing to do with whiskey. We have invaded a private person's home by mistake. Don't print anything you have written. Don't show any pictures you have taken. Because it's wrong."

I continued, "You're going to get the hell sued out of you if you do. Being a lawyer myself, I can practically guarantee that you're going to get the hell sued out of you. And if they call me as a witness, I am going to testify to that. I'm not going to get on a witness stand and lie and perjure myself."

The boys from *LIFE* protested. I said to them as forcefully as I could, "I'm telling you, forget it! We can find another time when you go on a raid."

A week or so later, someone handed me a copy of the new issue of *LIFE*. Lo and behold, staring out at me from its pages was our farmer in his underwear. *LIFE* had run a four-page spread on the failed raid. And to make matters worse, the guy was a deacon in the Baptist Church.

Several weeks later I got a visit from two lawyers from northeastern Oklahoma. They said they represented the old man and his wife, and they were going to sue *LIFE* magazine for libel and slander.

"Well, I knew it was coming," I said. "I just didn't know when."

They said, "Our client tells us that you told them that you made a mistake, that they shouldn't run any of this stuff, and if they did they might get themselves sued. Is that true?"

I answered, "Yes, that is true."

They did sue, and *LIFE* settled out of court for an undisclosed amount.

As embarrassing as the *LIFE* magazine fiasco seemed at the time, I am convinced that it was a big plus for our side. The publicity it generated helped to reinforce the myth I was trying to create.

Daily Oklahoman

In general, we did not get a lot of support from E.K. Gaylord, publisher of the *Daily Oklahoman*. He was a "dry" who backed Bill Atkinson in the primary against Edmondson. He knew that strict enforcement of liquor laws would lead to their repeal.

One item at issue was how much effort should we put into cracking down on moonshiners and their stills. We did relatively little still-busting because, in my view, they were too scattered out in the back woods and mountains.

But not wanting to leave any opportunity untapped, I made a special trip to Washington, D.C., to ask for help from the Alcohol and Tobacco Unit (ATU) in shutting down these operations. My request fit well with their goals inasmuch as moonshiners evaded paying taxes on the whiskey they sold. The head of the ATU promised full cooperation.

Therefore, it came as complete shock and dismay when I arrived back in Oklahoma City late that night and saw a newspaper headline that said the ATU had refused to help us.

It was already after midnight, but I drove by the governor's mansion and showed Howard the article. "What can we do about it?" I asked.

"Go tell Mr. Gaylord and ask him for his help," Howard responded.

I picked up the phone hesitatingly, given the lateness of the hour. My mind recalled some of the anti-Gaylord speeches I made during the campaign. But overcoming my trepidation, I dialed Mr. Gaylord's number. He answered the phone himself.

I told him that the headlines were wrong, that I had just returned from Washington and the ATU had agreed to help us.

Mr. Gaylord, rather than acting offended, said he was very sorry and he would do something about it.

The next day I learned he had called down to the plant and ordered them to stop the presses. He told his staff to rewrite the headline and story, and he ordered them to call the route drivers to pick up papers already delivered.

Although I may have had my differences with E.K. Gaylord, this incident proved he was a grand old man.

Raiding the Rich

A gaggle of critics were saying that our roadblocks and raids were only affecting the working class. They complained that we would never raid the rich. I got to thinking about that, and I decided I needed to show they were wrong.

Southern Hills Country Club in Tulsa was one of the richest places I knew. It had a big, beautiful club house and a championship golf course that hosted the U.S. Open. I knew they served a lot of whisky there.

To the surprise and chagrin of almost everyone connected with the club, I took a squad of troopers out there one night and conducted a raid on the rich and famous. No one was arrested, but we sure sent shock waves throughout the community. The message was that no one, no matter how rich, was exempt from Oklahoma's liquor laws.

Chatterbox Club

Pleased with the headlines generated by our raid on Southern Hills, I decided the time was ripe to step up the pressure on high-profile places.

The Chatterbox was one of the better night clubs in Oklahoma City. Located a block-and-a-half north of the state capitol on Lincoln Boulevard and across the street east from Beverly's Restaurant, it was a popular gathering place for lobbyists and state officials. The club was known for its big band music and dancing as well as fine dining. I happened to know also that alcohol could be bought there.

I sent two undercover agents to the club one Saturday night to observe what was going on. State law at the time said it was illegal for a person to be in a public place where drinking was taking place. My agents gathered evidence that alcohol was being served and consumed on the premises.

We arrived with a bevy of police and patrol cars. I stepped up onto the stage, motioned for the music to stop, and walked over to the microphone. I told the patrons that my name was Joe Cannon and this was a raid. "I have some bad news for you. You are all under arrest. Everyone here is under arrest."

Actually, I had no intention of filing charges on them. They were all good people. As a matter of fact, one was Paul Reed, my predecessor as commissioner of public safety. Mainly I wanted to draw high-level attention to our enforcement campaign.

When those words had sunk in, I continued with my spiel. "And then I have some further bad news for you. You are all going to jail."

A chorus of moans and groans rose to greet me. I surmised that more than one man was there with a lady other than his wife.

"There are enough police and highway patrol cars outside to take you all to jail," I stated. "I'm not going to let you drive yourselves down there. You are all going to be taken in police cars, and booked."

The chorus grew louder, accentuated by a few references to my parentage.

"The charge," I went on, "is congregating in a public place where liquor is being sold and drank."

When I finished talking, we had the patrons line up single file as they went out the front door to waiting police cars. I positioned myself just inside the door where they would have to walk past me. Some were ashen-faced and seemed on the verge of panic. The prospect of getting their names in the morning paper might cost them a job, a career, or perhaps an embarrassing explanation at home.

As each person passed, I said, "When you get down to the jail, they are going to fingerprint and book you as they would any common criminal, but I'm not trying to embarrass you. I've already told the booking officer that I don't care what name you give him. Whether you give your correct name or not is of no concern to me."

The next morning I learned that fifty men gave their name as Joe Cannon.

We booked 126 people that night. The only person not arrested was a twelve-year-old black lad who was back in the kitchen washing dishes. I told a highway patrolman, "Take that kid home. He is not going to jail."

The people were free to go after they had been booked and released. However, since the police did not provide two-way bus service, they had to get their own transportation back to their cars at the club or else call someone to come get them.

Every once in a while something falls between the cracks. This was one of those occasions. About three weeks later, I got a call from a jailer downtown. He said they still had a guy down there from the Chatterbox raid. *How can that be?* I thought. *We turned everybody loose.* It turned out that this guy was the band's drummer, he was new in town, and he didn't know anybody to call to come get him. I personally went down to the jail to pick him up and offer my apology.

He said, "Mr. Cannon, I can't be too mad at you. You put me in jail, but you also got me out."

Oklahoma City Golf & Country Club

I figured it would make bigger headlines and a bigger story if I raided the fabled Oklahoma City Golf and Country Club. That feat would be like bearding the lion in his own den. The club's membership roster read like a "Who's Who" of Oklahoma City society.

Moreover, I felt it would make a bigger impression if I conducted the raid entirely by myself.

Red lights flashing on my black Cadillac, I drove up the circular drive to the covered portico, got out, and strode through the big double-doors. On my left, I could see a balcony with a small bar on it where they were mixing drinks. People were milling around and drinking.

A young attendant came up to me. "Can I help you, sir?"

I said, "Yes you can. I want to see the manager."

"I'm sorry, but he's with a party that is going on in another part of the club. You'll have to wait awhile."

I gestured toward my mouth. "You watch my lips. I said, 'I want to see the manager.' I want to see him right now! And if you don't do that, you and the manager both are going to jail."

He snapped to attention.

"I am Joe Cannon," I added. "You probably have been hearing about me."

The boy scooted out of there, and in less than a minute he came back with the manager. I could see that he was absolutely beside himself.

I introduced myself and asked, "Didn't you get my letter?" I was referring to the letter I mailed to all the night clubs and hotels in the state.

"Yes, I got your letter, Commissioner. But I didn't take it seriously."

"Are you serving liquor in this club?"

"Yes, we have a bar." There was no way he could deny it because I could see for myself.

"Are people drinking in this place?"

"Yes."

"Well, I told you in my letter what I was going to do if you didn't stop. I gave you ample warning. So now, I am placing you under arrest." I pulled out a set of handcuffs and put them on his wrists.

The man's whole body started to shake. Apparently, this was his first arrest.

I paused as if changing my mind. "No, I'll tell you what I'm going to do. I will come back at seven o'clock in the morning with a whole bunch of law enforcement officers. We're going to search this place with a warrant. And if we find any liquor here, then I am going to file charges against you and every director of the Oklahoma City Golf and Country Club. You will be arrested and tried for violating the liquor laws of the State of Oklahoma."

He objected, "All the lockers in the men's and women's locker rooms are locked. I don't have a key to them. Only the member that has the locker has a key."

"Well, we'll just have to bring a pair of bolt-cutters and cut the locks off. One way or another, we're going to search every locker in the place."

That night, as it was reported to me, they held a meeting at 2:00 a.m. Every member they could find came to the meeting. If some man was out of town, his wife showed up. Some wore robes and nightclothes. They opened the lockers themselves, and if they didn't have a key they cut the lock.

To get rid of the liquor, they had the groundskeeper get out the backhoe and dig a deep trench somewhere on the far side of the property. Then they carried all the liquor out there, tossed it in the hole, and covered it up.

The place was as clean as a whistle when we showed up the next morning. No liquor was found anywhere.

I made a few more enemies out of that deal. But the story was splashed all over the newspapers, television, and radio. I did several media interviews.

The publicity proved to be very helpful as the campaign was building toward a climax.

Final Push

The vote on repeal was set for April 7. I told my troopers we dared not take anything for granted. It was important to keep the pressure on. So we conducted headlining raids and roadblocks clear up until the last day.

The climax came on Sunday, April 5, just two days before the election, when we launched our final big push. In the largest attack ever made on liquor, we marshaled 95 highway patrol officers who searched 3,253 vehicles in 39 roadblocks along the state's northern and eastern borders.

Concurrently, a team of 35 state, county, and city police officers from the Tulsa area were conducting raids of their own. They raided the homes of thirteen known bootleggers and fourteen night clubs.

When questioned about the massive effort, I facetiously told the press that I merely wanted to make sure Oklahomans were stone sober when they went to the polls on Tuesday.

Repeal passed handily. The final count was 396,845 to 314,380. Perhaps a more remarkable statistic is that a stunning 203,000 more citizens turned out for this election than the total number who voted in the governor's race.

Tribute to Gene Frusher

Gene Frusher was my idea of what a highway patrolman ought be. He stood about six-foot-four, weighed 225 pounds, and was tightly muscled. We had known each other since the late 1940s when he was stationed in Norman, Oklahoma, and I was attending law school there. From time to time he let me ride with him on patrol.

When I became head of the highway patrol in 1959, I had Gene transferred back to Oklahoma City from Guyman, where he was then stationed. He served as my driver and bodyguard for the three months I led the campaign to repeal prohibition, criss-crossing the state from Guyman to Grove and from Tonkawa to Tishomingo, putting in many twenty-hour days.

I told Gene I was going to form an elite squad of patrolmen, promote him to captain, and place him in charge of the new unit. They were to be called the Rescue Squad, and their mission was to help other law enforcement agencies in any emergency. To prepare them for their jobs, sent the team to New York for training in that city's highly acclaimed search and rescue school.

When informed that scuba diving was to be part of their training, Gene remarked, "What the hell is scuba diving?"

"You'll soon learn," I assured him.

He took the training and, so far as I know, became one of the first certified scuba divers in Oklahoma. Gene's squad was called upon to search lakes and rivers for evidence such as guns and knives used in the commission of a crime. I bought them boats to use in their work. That was the beginning of the Oklahoma Lake Patrol. Nowadays, almost all fire departments have scuba diving teams.

§ § §

6

Advising the Executive

The day after the prohibition referendum passed found me packing my desk for the move out to the capitol and the governor's office. I told Howard previously that as soon as the polls close, I'm through. I didn't want the commissioner's job forever; as a matter of fact, I didn't want it even for one extra day.

We named Ray Page to be the new commissioner of public safety. He had done such a good job as my number two man that we felt he was fully qualified to move up to the top slot.

It felt good to get back to lawyering. As First Legal Assistant to the Governor, my job was to do all the legal work for the office. I responded to legal filings, prepared extradition papers, and negotiated bond indentures.

Sam Crossland was the second lawyer in the office. Sam had been an assistant DA under Howard in Tulsa. He stood about five-foot-five, medium build, wore his hair close-clipped, and was very funny. He could have made a nice living as a professional entertainer.

One time Sam accompanied Howard and me to a meeting of the Oil Compact Commission in Scottsdale, Arizona. That night we went to a club in downtown Scottsdale, and the entertainment was a singer-piano player. When the entertainer took a break, Howard nudged Sam and said, "Why don't you go up there and play while the man is gone?"

Sam did. He played the piano and sang old-time western songs

like "Riding Old Paint," "If Dogs Have a Heaven," and "Bury
Me Not on the Lone Prairie." He drew great applause.

Pretty soon, the club's entertainer came back from his break.
But instead of going up on stage, he sat down at our table with us.
"I want to sit here and enjoy him," he said. "He's something."

He asked if Sam was a professional. I said, "No, he's a
lawyer."

Liaison with the Legislature

I examined every piece of legislation that came across the
governor's desk. Then I'd make a recommendation to Howard.
Most of the time he followed my advice because I had previously
been in the legislature myself and knew the procedures.

Often a legislator would come by the office to show me an
amendment he wanted to introduce. They wanted to know, was it
in line with the governor's thinking? I'd give them my
interpretation.

I played an active role in helping Howard pick out the leaders
of the legislature. Back then, the governor designated who was
going to be the speaker of the house. We picked Clint Livingston
from Marietta. In so doing, we passed over J.D. McCarty, who
was the front-runner for the job. J.D. was an imposing figure; he
could have doubled for the character Ralph Cramden on "The
Honeymooners" television series. He had a bigger following in
the legislature and exercised more power than did our man, and
the legislative gang wanted him to be their speaker. But we didn't
think J.D. was honest. (Note: Several years later, McCarty went to
jail on tax evasion charges.)

We chose three men to be floor leaders. Their role was to bring
down the bills the governor wanted introduced. They also rounded
up support for or against bills the governor either endorsed or
opposed.

One of the floor leaders we chose was Frank Ogden. He later
became a district judge in western Oklahoma and tried to block
my ruling on the School Land Commission.

Jack-of-All-Trades

Every governor needs a jack-of-all-trades to "carry his water" for him, so to speak. Some people might term this a "hatchet man." Whether jack-of-all trades or hatchet man, I carried a lot of water in the Edmondson administration.

Getting rid of patronage employees was one of the most onerous tasks. Typical of the situation was a request by State Representative Noble Stewart. He came to Howard with a list of patronage employees of Senator Ray Fine in Sequoyah County that he wanted fired and replaced with his own people. Howard handed the list to me and said, "See what you can do."

Immediately, I perceived a dilemma. On the one hand, Stewart was a loyal Edmondson supporter and was our election representative in Sallisaw. Fine, on the other hand, was generally against us; however, he was the most powerful senator in the legislature and in a position to block approval of our key legislative programs.

Both men were important to our legislative agenda. It was incumbent on me, therefore, to handle the situation in such a way as not to antagonize both.

Unfortunately, one of the people I fired was Ray Fine's blind brother. I sought out Fine and apologized, "I just want you to know one thing. I didn't know your brother was blind."

He replied graciously, "I know that, I know you wouldn't do that."

Thus, I managed to avoid a falling-out over that incident.

Occasionally some legislator would go a little too far. Noble Stewart was one of these. He approached Leland Gourley one day and said he wanted us to put his daughter on the payroll, but give her nothing to do. She would, in effect, be a "ghost employee." We wouldn't do it. Noble got ticked off at us at first, but later he got over it.

Most of the time, however, I worked through the appropriate department heads such as Lloyd Rader at the welfare agency or John Doolin, highway commissioner. All department heads knew that when I called them, it was really Howard calling. I could call

Lloyd Rader and say, "Fire John Brown." He'd say, "Okay." He wouldn't ask me why.

Lloyd Rader was a great personality. Tall, gaunt, craggy-faced with a full head of unruly hair, he exercised a tremendous influence with the legislature. He could help put a project across. In fact, if it weren't for Rader's muscle, we wouldn't have been able to get enough votes through the legislature to authorize such major projects as the H.E. Bailey Turnpike and Kerr Dam. His source of power lay in the fact that most of the people on his payroll were patronage employees of the various state senators and representatives.

Rader took a lot of criticism. Personally, I think he was completely honest. He did a fine job running the welfare agency. He knew what his limitations were. And he knew he held a political job. If the governor wanted somebody hired or fired, Rader saw to it that they got hired or fired.

Central Purchasing

One of Howard's campaign promises was to establish a central purchasing system for the state. Hundreds of separate state purchasing agents were causing duplication of effort and waste of state money. There was no standardization of contracts, no competitive bidding, and no pooling of purchasing power.

We found, for example, that some departments were paying ten times as much for stationary as was another department.

In another case, I discovered after I took over the highway patrol that for years, every highway patrol car was purchased from a tiny Ford dealership in Madill, Oklahoma. It was just a coincidence, I guess, that former governor Raymond Gary lived in Madill.

I learned from Highway Commissioner John Doolin that all the wooden stakes used as markers in highway construction--and the state purchased millions--all came from one little lumber yard. Guess where? In Madill, Oklahoma. No bids. Every one of them was purchased from one damned little lumber yard.

Mike Pedrick and Carl Bates headed up the effort to design the system. We came up with a deal where any purchase over $200 had to go through central purchasing. They would buy it for the individual agency, and because they had the purchasing power of buying for other departments that needed the same thing, they could buy it at a much lower price...normally on a competitive bid basis. It saved the state millions of dollars.

We had a struggle getting it through the legislature. State agencies, elected officials, salesmen, and merchants selling to the state all fought it. Higher education was the biggest holdout; we had to do a trade-off with the universities, but eventually we got the bill passed.

Carl Bates from Muskogee was our choice to be chairman of the Central Purchasing Commission. He was well-known, highly regarded, very honest, and a damned good businessman.

Merit System

Another of Howard's campaign promises was to establish a merit system for state employees. Most state employees--some estimates ran as high as ninety percent--were patronage appointees of some state official, such as the governor, an elected agency head, or a legislator.

Senator Ray Fine from Gore probably had more people on the patronage payroll than any other senator, and possibly more than all other senators combined. Moreover, the Fine group was a political enemy of the Edmondson group, of which I was a card-carrying member. In the past, I had several encounters with him during my time in the legislature.

On the plus side, Fine was one of those people who's word was always good. If he promised you something, you could take it to the bank.

The governor called me into his office one day. He said his bill on the merit system was coming up for a vote in the senate, and the outcome was very much in doubt. "I want you to go down to Gore and talk to Fine about voting for the bill."

"You have got to be kidding!"

He said, "No, I'm serious. I want you to talk to Senator Fine."

"Howard, you had me fire a bunch of people put on the state payroll by Senator Fine. My God, I even fired Senator Fine's blind brother."

As usual, Howard talked me into it. After all, what else could I do. The worst that could happen would be for Fine to say no.

I telephoned Senator Fine on the weekend at his home in Gore. I said, "I want to come down and talk with you."

He said, "Come on."

The senator came out to meet me as I drove up the driveway to his house. "Don't get out," he said. "I want you to drive me somewhere."

He got in my car and directed me where to drive. We drove all over the backwoods of Sequoyah County. Finally, he had me stop the car in a densely-wooded area. We got out and climbed over a four-strand barbed wire fence.

We came to a little clearing. The senator seemed very much at peace here. "What did you want to see me about?" he asked.

I talked for a while about the merit system, what it would do for state employees, and said we wanted him to vote for the bill. To my utter surprise, he said he would.

Monday morning, when I got back to the governor's office, I told Howard and other members of the staff that Senator Fine was going to vote for the bill. They just laughed.

True to his word, when the clerk called for the vote, Senator Fine answered, "Aye." You could have heard a pin drop in the senate chamber.

Why had he voted our way? My best guess is that he was a shrewd operator. He found a way to protect the large number of patronage people he still had on the payroll. In other words, by establishing a merit system for state employees, he would "grandfather" these people, and thus their positions would be secure no matter what political games were played in the future.

Constitutional Highway Commission

Edmondson's success in getting central purchasing and an employee merit system did not carry over to another of his campaign promises, namely, a constitutional highway commission.

His idea was to remove the governor and legislators from the highway construction program. The current system was ripe for graft, greed, and corruption.

Howard proposed an eight-member commission that would come from their respective districts, would serve staggered terms of eight years, and could be removed only for cause. The objective was an independent commission that could execute a long-range program devoid of politics.

Giving up their privileged position was more than the legislators could stomach. They allowed the bill for a constitutional amendment to die an ignoble death.

Interstate 35. If we had a constitutional highway commission such as Edmondson proposed, we might have avoided a knock-down, drag-out battle over the routing of Interstate 35 to Dallas. Senator Joe Bailey Cobb, Tishomingo, wanted the interstate to go through Tishomingo, twenty miles east of its present route. The initial design called for a straight shot through the Arbuckle Mountains. He held up approval of I-35 for a couple of years.

We couldn't talk Senator Cobb out of it. I tried. Lord knows I tried. But he was not swayed by figures that showed a road-cut through the Arbuckles was much cheaper than the routing he wanted.

Ultimately, it took the muscle of the federal government, combined with the presence of Bob Kerr in the senate and Ed Edmondson in the house, to build up enough pressure to break Cobb's legislative logjam.

The key can be found in a parody on the Golden Rule, namely, "He who has the gold makes the rule." In this case, 90 percent of the cost of building the interstate would be paid by the U.S. Government, 10 percent by Oklahoma. (Note: The ratio is 50-50 for building state roads.)

Accordingly, government highway engineers were not willing to put up 90 percent of the additional cost of going through downtown Tishomingo. They said, "Go south!"

Curing Corruption

We also said we were going to clean up the county commissioners. We tried, but we couldn't get anything done because nobody would help us. We couldn't get any district attorneys to cooperate.

For example, Howard sent me down to Purcell, county seat of McClain County. Citizens asked for the governor's help in exposing corruption in their commissioner's office. Howard sent me down there to check out the situation. We found that one commissioner had spent hundreds of thousands of dollars in a two-day period for new bridge timbers. We looked around the commission yard but weren't able to find any timbers.

I confronted him.

He said, "They have all been put on bridges."

"But the invoice says there were hundreds of new bridge timbers."

"They put them out yesterday."

I asked him to take me out to a bridge and show me one new timber.

He said, "Son, I ain't got time to do that."

Getting nowhere on that front, I then asked him about another invoice that showed he paid thousands of dollars to a trucker for hauling gravel. He refused to answer.

I went out and located the trucker. He told me he did not own a truck and had not hauled any gravel. Next, I went to the bank. The banker told me that the commissioner brought a big check into the bank each month; he would endorse the "ghost" trucker's name and pocket the money.

We had the goods on two of the commissioners. No question about it. When I took the information to the district attorney, he called me into his office. "Go back to Oklahoma City," he said.

"The grand jury is going to indict you."

"Go ahead and indict me," I told him. "But before you can get the sheriff up here to take me to jail, I'll have a pardon from the governor. We worked this out before I came down here. Besides that, I'll call the highway patrol, and we'll have more highway patrolmen down here than you know what to do with. Now what are you going to do about it?"

He backed down. "Well, I guess I'm not going to do anything about it."

McClain County was not an isolated instance. We found evidence of corruption in other counties as well. Again, we couldn't get anybody to help us. The system was too entrenched. It was the "good-old-boy" system in operation. Many commissioners viewed these things as perks of the job.

Ultimately, it took the FBI and the federal government to do anything about it.

Nix Tricks

On the day of the scheduled execution of Pete Williams, the guy whom Howard, as Tulsa DA, had convicted of kidnapping the young divinity student, Williams' attorneys asked for an extension to file a new appeal. The governor granted them one week.

He called me at my office to inform me of the extension. It was about four in the afternoon. A bunch of media people were there, including Otis Sullivant, dean of the capitol news corps.

Howard said, "Don't execute Pete Williams tonight because I have given the lawyers a week to file their new claim."

I told Sam Crossland, "You'd better call Ray Page [warden] and tell him." Page, who took my place as commissioner of public safety, was now warden of the prison at McAlester where the execution would take place.

Sam just kept sitting there and sitting there. Finally, Otis couldn't stand it any longer. He said, "Sam, aren't you going to call Ray Page?"

Sam said, "Oh, I'm kinda busy. I'll call him tomorrow."

He was just joking, of course. But it really shook up Otis.

The appeal failed, and Williams' execution was reset. We went into our regular routine for the night of an execution. About 11:30 p.m., Sam Crossland and I went over to the Governor's Mansion. Sam and I were in a room with two telephones. The governor and his wife were in another room.

To make sure there were no mistakes, I had the warden on his walk-around phone. I instructed him, "Don't you get off that phone until this is over with, because I'm sitting here beside the governor in the governor's mansion."

We kept a second line open in case an emergency call came in.

About ten minutes to midnight, we got a call on the second line. The caller identified himself as Kirksey Nix, chief justice of the Court of Criminal Appeals. He said he was issuing a stay of execution.

Only two people have the authority to stay an execution, the governor of the state and the chief justice of the Court of Criminal Appeal.

I yelled at Sam, "Go get the governor. Kirksey Nix is on the phone. He's issuing a stay of execution."

While Sam was going after the governor, I talked to Warden Page on the other line. "We got a call from Judge Nix, and under no circumstances is the prisoner to be executed. Don't do anything until you hear from me. Do you understand?"

He said he did. I had him repeat it back. The killer was already strapped in the chair. Execution was about two minutes away.

The governor came to the phone and talked to Justice Nix. He turned to me, "That's not Kirksey Nix! I know Kirksey's voice."

We went ahead with the execution as scheduled.

A few days later, we learned that the caller was Jimmy Nix, the judge's brother.

What a prank!

Death of Senator Kerr

Senator Robert S. Kerr died unexpectedly on New Year's Day, 1963. Oklahoma University was playing Alabama in the Orange Bowl, the outcome of which would determine the national champion. Howard Edmondson was in the final two weeks of his term. He flew a party of 30 administration officials in a National Guard plane to see the game. We stopped on the way to pick up Fritz Hollings, governor of South Carolina, and his wife, Pat.

President Kennedy also came down to Miami for the game. He sat in a private box on the fifty-yard line, well guarded by a cadre of Secret Service men. Our group, on the other hand, had a block of regular stadium seats about twenty yards away.

The football players were just coming onto the field when a Secret Service agent came over to where we were sitting. He asked for the governor. "The President wants you to send one of your trusted people over. He needs to talk to him."

Howard sent me. I went up to the President's box. The Secret Service men were very protective of him. They gave me a thorough body-pat search before allowing me to enter. Jack made room for me to sit down beside him.

"Yes, Mr. President. What can I do for you?" I asked.

He appeared solemn. "First, are you an attorney?"

I answered yes.

"Then I want you to know our conversation is confidential."

"Yes, sir."

"Joe, have you heard that Bob Kerr is dead?"

"Yes, sir. We heard it just a few minutes ago."

"You go tell Howard that I want him to take Bob Kerr's place. Tell him he needs to resign from office and have the lieutenant governor appoint him to the senate."

I carried the message back to Howard. He said, "Tell the President that my answer is no."

I trotted back up to the President's box. He refused to accept Howard's answer. He said, "Tell him I want him in the senate."

Off I went again to the Oklahoma section. Howard was still adamant.

Back to the President's box. He said, "Tell Howard to think of what we can do for Oklahoma with him in the senate, his brother Ed in the house, and me in the Presidency."

Each time I went to the President's box--it must have been seven or eight times--the Secret Service subjected me to a thorough search. Finally, I asked, "Mr. President, would you please have the Secret Service look at my face and recognize me when I come back? I'm tired of being searched."

He called them over and said, "Let this man through when he comes back."

Howard's mind was not convinced by the President's argument. He expressed concern about possible political repercussions within Oklahoma.

I relayed Howard's message to the President. He sounded disappointed. "We will talk about it again in a day or two," he said. "Right now, let's watch the game."

It was halftime by the time I got back to my seat. I had missed seeing the entire first half.

Howard sent me to telephone Lieutenant Governor George Nigh back in Oklahoma. With the governor out of the state, the lieutenant governor had full power to make appointments, including filling the vacancy to the U.S. Senate. It was important that Edmondson reassure Nigh and keep him on the reservation.

It took me fifteen minutes in that big arena to find a concession with a telephone and get a pocket-full of quarters. Then I spent nearly an hour chasing down George Nigh on a New Year's holiday. I located him at his mother's home in McAlester.

Mine wasn't the first call. George had already heard the news. As a matter of fact, he got a call from a state senator who was profoundly disappointed to learn he was not at the game with the rest of us. Had Nigh been out of the state, the opportunity to name a new U.S. senator would have fallen to the president pro-tem of the state senate.

George assured me that as far as he was concerned he was only the *acting* governor, that Howard was still the governor even though he was in Florida. He said he had no intention of naming anyone to the U.S. Senate; that was a decision for Howard to make.

He asked me what the score of the game was. I told him I didn't know, as I had not had an opportunity to watch a single play.

I returned to our section with my report. Howard was happy to receive George Nigh's assurance. I sat down to watch the rest of the game.

The game was over. Oklahoma lost 17 to 0.

I was probably the first person to travel all the way to Miami to watch the University of Oklahoma play for the national championship in the Orange Bowl, and miss the entire game.

The day after Kerr's funeral, Howard took the U.S. Senate seat. A lot of people complained he should have offered it to Grayce Kerr, the senator's widow, to fill out her husband's term. In fact, Howard did call her, but she declined. He then offered it to Robert Kerr, Jr., the senator's son, who was ambivalent. Ed Edmondson also turned down the offer, preferring to retain his secure seat in the House of Representatives. With nine days left in his term, Howard resigned the governorship and, in a pre-arranged ceremony, had George Nigh sign the certificate of appointment.

Howard's political instinct proved correct. Many Oklahomans reacted as he feared: they viewed his self-appointment as a power grab. He went from being a "fair-haired" governor to becoming a "black sheep" senator. He lost his bid for reelection two years later.

§ § §

7

Fraternizing with the Famous

The governor's office was a great place to meet the rich and famous. Especially Edmondson's office. Howard had a great knack for attracting celebrities. By virtue of being his right-hand man, I fraternized with a lot of people I otherwise would not have met. They ranged from football stars like Billy Vessels (1952 Heisman Trophy winner), to movie stars like Dale Robertson, to recording stars like Patti Page and Connie Stevens, to political powerhouses like Carl Albert and Robert S. Kerr. It was usually my job to take care of visiting dignitaries.

Whenever anybody important came to town, Howard would have them over to a reception at the Governor's Mansion. That's how I met actors Glenn Ford and Maria Schell while they were here filming the movie, "Cimarron." Another time, songwriter Hoagie Carmichael was at the mansion playing the piano. We sat up half the night playing the piano and singing nostalgic songs.

Usually, after most of the public had gone home, we'd have an after-party for the favored few, usually at some popular restaurant like Vic and Honey's.

Actor-director Jose Ferrer came to town in 1962 with cast and crew to shoot the movie, "State Fair." The cast included such luminaries as Pat Boone, Ann-Margaret, Bobby Darin, David Brandon, Tom Ewell, and Alice Faye.

Howard held a reception for the cast at the mansion. The men all drooled over Ann-Margaret. She was really, really good-looking. Great, great figure, and flaming red hair.

We all went to Vic and Honey's for dinner. The owners had previously been in vaudeville and knew Jose Ferrer. I was seated next to Jose at the same table. I said something that I wish I hadn't said. (I've been known to do that before.) Somehow, it came up in conversation that he had just won the Academy Award for his role in "Cyrano de Bergerac."

He asked me, "Did you see the picture."

"Yes, I did see the picture," I replied. "But I don't think you should have won the Academy Award."

He looked surprised. "Well, who do you think should have won it?"

"William Holden for his role in 'Sunset Boulevard.'"

Now it was my turn to be surprised. "I agree with you," Jose said. "It wasn't anything for me to play Cyrano de Bergerac. I had played the role so many times on the stage, that it wasn't any challenge for me to do it in the movie."

He continued, "But the part that William Holden played, that was a real challenge. So to tell you the truth, I agree with you."

John F. Kennedy

Howard got a call in the spring of 1960 from then Senator John F. Kennedy, asking him to come up to Washington for a private meeting. Howard said yes.

The call didn't come as any great surprise. Congressman Ed Edmondson had been working behind the scenes to set it up. Kennedy was then involved in the race for the Democratic nomination for president, and he was trying to line up as many governors as possible to be his campaign managers in their own states. Most Oklahomans were leaning toward Lyndon Johnson of Texas. Kennedy wanted Howard to be his campaign manager for Oklahoma.

Howard, Ed and I went to Kennedy's home in the Georgetown section of Washington, D.C. He had the damnedest magnetism about him. When he first greeted us, I just stood in awe. He was so magnetic. It was hard at first to say anything to him. As a matter of fact, I personally didn't have much to say because most of the conversation took place between him, the governor, and the congressman.

Kennedy started off by saying he wanted us to help him in the campaign. We pledged our support to his candidacy.

The conversation carried on to the lunch hour. His wife, Jackie, came down the stairs bearing a tray of lunch for us. She was simply attired in a blouse and blue jeans. Undoubtedly, she was one of the most attractive women I have ever seen. Her pictures didn't do her justice. She had a magnetism about her just as powerful as Jack had.

Jack said he'd be letting us know what we could do to help, and so forth and so on. Everything Howard became involved in, I became involved in. So in Jack Kennedy's mind, Howard and I were his two top people in Oklahoma.

Later on, Kennedy asked Howard to be one of the speakers who seconded his nomination.

Jack gave us his private White House telephone number. We could call up and get him on the phone if we wanted to. The Secret Service knew who we were and always put our calls through without delay.

Howard made an appointment for us to talk with him about the Markham Ferry Dam, which involved refinancing some of the state's debt. But we had been blocked by petty bureaucrats all up and down the line.

The night before our appointment, Howard and I stayed in the Roosevelt Hotel. After dinner, we repaired to our room to sip some good brandy. The more brandy we sipped, the more fertile our brains became--or so it seemed. Before the evening was over, we had figured out what the country ought to do about its troubles in the Middle East...and all the other hot spots around the world.

Howard and I both agreed we ought to call Jack Kennedy and tell him what he could do to solve those problems. So Howard said, "Go get him on the phone."

I had the President's direct phone number, so I called him. It was about two o'clock in the morning.

The Secret Service man answered. I told him who I was. "I'm from Oklahoma City. I'm a lawyer for the governor."

He asked, "Is Governor Edmondson with you?" (He knew who we were.)

I said, "Yes. We need to talk to the President. We've got some things we need to tell him."

"Won't they wait until in the morning?"

I insisted, "No, it's very important. It has to do with what the government ought to do overseas in some real trouble spots."

"But don't you have an appointment with him in the morning in the Oval Office?"

I said, "Yes, but we need to tell him now."

"Well, you know it's two o'clock in the morning, don't you?"

"Oh yeah, I know that. We just need to talk to him."

He said, "Well...if you really want me to, I'll go wake the President."

I turned to Howard. "Howard, do you think we really ought to do this?"

Howard thought a moment. "No. Tell him thanks anyway, but we'll just wait and talk to him in the morning."

Morning came. We went to the Oval Office. As he greeted us, Kennedy smiled and said, "I hear you guys were in your cups last night."

We laughed and said, "Yes, Mr. President."

"What was it you were going to tell me?"

"Yes sir, we had solved all your overseas problems, but we're not as sure about our solutions this morning as we were last night."

Howard and I told Jack about the troubles we had been having with the bureaucrats on the Markham Ferry Dam. The key to the project was refinancing the state's turnpike debt. The bond houses were all for the idea--in fact, they were the ones who proposed it. But everywhere we turned we ran into bureaucratic obstacles.

Kennedy said, "Here's what I want you to do. When you get back to Oklahoma City, you start off where you did before, and this time you might get a different answer."

Sure enough, he was right. We started at the lowest bureaucrat and worked our way up the ladder. At each level, they suddenly said, "That's a wonderful idea."

Thanks to JFK, Markham Ferry Dam and Lake (now Kerr Dam and Hudson Lake) became a reality.

Frank Sinatra

During Kennedy's election campaign, Howard came up with the damnedest idea. We would put together a team built around Frank Sinatra to go around to major college campuses and campaign for Jack. He figured we could draw great crowds if Sinatra were to put on a concert, following which Howard would make a campaign speech for Kennedy. My job was to handle the arrangements.

Frank, as we already knew, was a Kennedy enthusiast. (Jack had mentioned that when we were in Georgetown.) Howard found out Sinatra was performing in Atlantic City. We had a trip to Washington lined up. So he made arrangements that when we finished our business, we would go on down to Atlantic City to see Sinatra.

He called Sinatra. He told him he was the Governor of Oklahoma and that we wanted to talk about the Kennedy campaign. "We have a plan, and we want to ask you about it."

Sinatra replied, "Fine, come on down." He even told us the name of the hotel where he was staying.

Getting from Washington to Atlantic City turned out to be more of a chore than we thought. We couldn't get an airplane, so we had to ride the Greyhound bus. The distance wasn't far, but it took us practically all night to get there.

As soon as we checked in at the hotel, Howard called Sinatra's room. He had a little trouble getting through the hotel operator, who apparently had orders to screen callers, but eventually he got through. Frank invited us to come down to watch the show that evening, and then we'd talk.

He sent a limousine to pick us up. We were taken around to the back stage entrance, ushered into the show room, and seated at a ringside table. It was probably my imagination, but I could just see everybody asking, who in the hell are those guys?

Frank invited us back to his dressing room after the show. It was set with a table of hors d'oeuvres.

After mingling with well-wishers and hangers-on for a while, we rode back to the hotel with Frank and went up to his room. Howard told him what the plan was.

Frank said, "I think that sounds great!"

"I hoped you might like it," Howard said.

"Not only will I be there," Frank said, "but I'll bring Nelson Riddle's band to provide the music."

We left it with that and went back home.

Howard called Jack Kennedy, who said he thought it was a great idea. He said he'd get back to us.

Jack called back a few hours later. "The deal is off," he said. It was vetoed by his brother Bobby, who was his campaign manager. Bobby was afraid that since the press was always trying to link Sinatra to the Mafia, that sort of image could be bad for the campaign.

Howard called me into his office and explained the situation. He was profoundly disappointed. "You call Frank and tell him what happened," he said.

I called Sinatra's number and told him what Bobby said. Frank became very angry that Bobby would do that to him, considering how strongly he had plugged for Jack. (Note: I think this was the start of the rupture between Sinatra and the Kennedy White House.)

We visited for a while. Frank began to calm down. I told him how much I appreciated what he was going to do for us.

Somehow the subject of golf came up. He mentioned that he lived next door to a golf course. I told him I had recently taken up the game. He asked what my handicap was. I told him it was a five.

He asked me if I played in any tournaments. I told him that it had always been my dream to play in the Bing Crosby Pro-Am at Pebble Beach.

He said, "You want to play in that?"

I replied, "I'd love to."

"Then don't worry about it," he said. "You will be in."

About a week later, I got an engraved invitation in the mail from Bing Crosby to play in the Bing Crosby tournament.

The tournament was played the last weekend in the January 1961. It was first time in the history of the tournament that it snowed. We had to delay play one day because the greens were covered with snow.

I was teamed with a no-name pro. But I didn't care. I met some wonderful people there. I played almost as good as my pro did. If I'd had a good pro, we'd have had a chance in the pro-am part.

Sinatra called my home one time. Caroline answered the phone. He said, "Happy birthday, Caroline. This is Frank Sinatra."

She bubbled, "You didn't have to tell me. I knew who it was as soon as I heard your voice." His call absolutely thrilled her to death.

Sinatra called me in December 1963 when his son was kidnapped. The boy, 19, was abducted at Lake Tahoe, drugged, and transported in the trunk of a car.

He phoned the house. I wasn't there. I was staying at a motel in Pryor, Oklahoma, while working on condemnation proceedings for land for the Markham Ferry Dam. It was late at night and I was asleep.

Caroline told him where I could be reached. When the call came through, the motel clerk rang my room and said, "Mr. Cannon, I hate to wake you up, but there's a man on the phone who says he's Frank Sinatra. Do you think that could be true?"

I said, "Yes, ma'am, that could be true. Put him through."

He told me about his son being kidnapped, and he said he wanted some legal advice.

The first thing I asked was, "Tell me first, Frank, was he really kidnapped? Or is it a publicity stunt?" (This would not have been the first time a celebrity's offspring had faked a kidnap.)

"No, it's for real, Joe."

I told him, "Check out and see if they have a good United

States Attorney in Nevada. See if he's a good lawyer and a good prosecutor. If he's not top-notch, hire some top-notch lawyers to sit in with the U.S. Attorney and give him some advice about things to do and not do."

I told him if he wanted me to, I'd come out there.

He said, "I think I can handle it."

I said, "I'm sure you've got some top-notch lawyers on your payroll. Being who you are, I'm sure you've got some damned good lawyers."

That was the last time I talked to Frank.

His son was ransomed three days later for $240,000).

Harry S. Truman

I was in Jefferson City, Missouri, in 1961 as part of the Oklahoma delegation to the funeral of James T. Blair, Missouri's governor who died in a tragic home accident. Jim Blair and I had been very good friends.

Former President Harry Truman was among the mourners. He impressed me as being a surprisingly ordinary-looking man, nearly eighty, remarkably spry and alert, and who looked at you with a penetrating gaze.

A number of us gathered in the library at Blair's home. Ed was in there. Howard was in there. Harry Truman was in there. And maybe a dozen more. This was my first time to see President Truman in person.

For some reason unbeknownst to me, all the others left the room to go to some other part of the house. Only two people remained in the library, me and Harry Truman.

I didn't know what to say. Truman, on the other hand, seemed content not to say anything. In fact, he had a half-smile on his face, as if enjoying my discomfort.

Unable to keep quiet any longer, I took it upon myself to break the silence. I told him who I was, that I was the legal assistant to Governor Edmondson, and I said, "Mr. President, I am an ex-marine. I spent almost four years in the Marine Corps--two-and-a-half years overseas. When you dropped the bomb on

Hiroshima, we were back in the States loading ships with our equipment--guns, ammunition, everything--getting ready to invade Japan. You dropped the bomb on Hiroshima, and when you dropped the bomb on Nagasaki they threw in the towel...and suddenly the war was over.''

He nodded in understanding.

I went on, ''I really think I owe my life to you. I made it through two-and-a-half years of combat without getting hurt, but I knew--a bunch of us knew--that we'd never make it through the invasion of Japan.''

He nodded again. People were beginning to drift back into the room. I hastened to conclude.

''I want to ask you a question. You may not want to answer it, but I'd like to ask it as an old marine sergeant. When you dropped the first bomb--there's been so many stories about what you thought and felt--I'd just like to ask you personally, was it a big decision? A tremendous, hard decision to make?''

He looked at me just as straight as an arrow. ''Son, I thought of how many young American boys were going to die invading Japan....'' He paused, then stated with emphasis, '''Tweren't no decision at all.''

Those were his exact words. I'll never forget them as long as I live. '''Tweren't no decision at all.''

I said, ''Well, Mr. President, I want you to know I appreciate you. A whole bunch of other marines I know do also. We thank you.''

§ § §

8

Running for Governor

In 1970, Oklahoma Democrats had been chafing under eight years of Republican dominance of the governorship. First, there was Henry Bellmon who succeeded Edmondson. Then there was Dewey F. Bartlett who, in my opinion, was a do-nothing governor. Lacking strong leadership at the top, the state was falling behind the nation in the economy, education and transportation.

I took stock of myself. Number one, I had widespread name recognition from my days of busting prohibition. Second, I had four years experience as a governor's right-hand man. And third, I was fired with zeal to carry on the reforms initiated by Howard Edmondson.

On the liability side of the ledger, I was stuck the nickname "Whiskey Joe" from my whiskey raiding days. I didn't like it, but the name just wouldn't go away. Also, I had a very meager war chest--and since money is the mother's milk of politics, that put me at a disadvantage.

Nevertheless, hope springs eternal, as some like to say. So, fueled mainly by hope and little else, I threw my hat in the ring. We hoped that the public would quickly rally to our cause and open their purse strings.

Edmondson Weighs Comeback

Howard Edmondson was devastated when he lost his bid for reelection to the U.S. Senate in 1966. He entered private law practice in Oklahoma City. He and I worked together on several cases.

Howard talked like he wanted to make a political comeback, and many Democrats were trying to persuade him to seek the governorship again. He made overtures toward entering the 1970 campaign. He had a campaign committee set up. There was no question that he wanted to run. He told me he was going to run.

We were on a plane to Denver to argue the school segregation ruling before the 10th Circuit Court of Appeal. He and I were the lawyers for the school people opposing busing. Howard was the lead attorney, but I was the one who argued the case. We lost.

Howard just flat out told me, in his customarily direct way, "When we get back home, I want you to withdraw from the governor's race."

I said, "F____ you."

We didn't have a very pleasant trip out there and back after that little round.

I felt a little resentful. I had done everything he ever wanted me to do for years. If Howard had sat down and talked to me, I might have agreed to withdraw. But when he just told me to get out, he got my dander up. There was no way I was going to quit now.

The filing period opened June 6 to 8. Howard elected not to run. He never told me why, but in my own mind I like to think it may have been out of regard for me. We had been the closest of friends since childhood, and through the years I had subordinated my political aspirations to his. Perhaps he thought it was my turn to have a "place in the sun."

Campaign Platform

I ran on a reform platform. Many of the things I wanted to do were the same things Howard sought but failed to get when he was in the governor's chair. One of them was a constitutional highway commission.

Another was a liquor-by-the-drink law. This would be the logical extension of our repeal of prohibition. The existing law was all but unenforcible, and consequently it was widely ignored.

We had *de facto* liquor by the drink. Everybody knew it. I just thought it would be better to have it regulated.

I preached a two-pronged approach toward the liquor-by-the-drink issue: *taxation* and *control.*

The loss of tax revenues was a big part of the argument. Bars that sold mixed drinks illegally did not pay tax on the liquor they dispensed. Not only were tax revenues not coming in, but the ability of bars and clubs to keep operating under the nose of the law usually depended on bribing sheriffs and other law enforcement officials.

Hence, the present system tended to be a cause of corruption and bribery of public officials. Whereas the retail liquor stores--being regulated--were very careful about who they sold liquor to, the bars tended to sell to anyone, including minors.

Campaign contribution reform was also high on my agenda. I was dead set against the political action committees. I thought it wrong to bring in out-of-state money.

Primary Opponents

My opponents in the Democratic primary were David Hall, Bryce Baggett, and Wilburn Cartwright. All came into the race with strong name recognition. Baggett was a state senator from Oklahoma City. Cartwright was a corporation commissioner and former U.S. Congressman. Hall was a former district attorney of Tulsa County who had made a strong showing in the 1966 governor's race.

Baggett and Cartwright, by virtue of their positions as state senator and corporation commissioner, could always find ways to keep their names before the public. Hall had a knack for generating publicity about himself. The media adored him. I, on the other hand, was saddled with the nickname,"Whiskey Joe." News stories almost invariably tagged me with that moniker.

David Hall was a tremendous speaker, renowned for his phenomenal capacity for remembering people's names. He never met a person he couldn't call by name years later. A handsome, well-exercised father of three he was a hulking man of forty with a flowing mane of prematurely white hair and an infectious grin. He was extremely popular with the press, which practically gave him the election from the start.

Hall had an almost insurmountable head start on the rest of us. Almost as soon as his 1966 race ended, he indicated he would try again for the governorship in 1970. For the next four years, he criss-crossed the state speaking at countless civic clubs and Democratic gatherings, building a county-by-county organization, and raising funds for his campaign war chest. His campaign was fueled by a nearly inexhaustible supply of money.

Campaign Tactics

My campaign was a pretty mundane affair. I had a hard time raising money. Without enough funds to buy television time, I was pretty much limited to running around the state passing out cards, putting up signs, talking to civic groups, and so forth. Occasionally, I'd get a television news clip.

Running a "poor boy" campaign had many unforseen consequences. One afternoon, I was driving back from Edmond in an ancient Cadillac we owned. That Cadillac was a great car for campaigning because it had a trunk big enough to carry a couple dozen campaign signs and posts. I could often be seen putting up my own signs.

I stopped at a vacant lot where the owner had given me permission to put up a sign. I put the car in park and left the engine idling while I took the sign, the post and the posthole digger out of the trunk. By now, I had honed the business of putting up signs to a fine art.

But something went awry this time. Just as I started digging the hole the car started moving away from me. Apparently, I didn't have the shift lever all the way into the park position.

I chased after it, thinking, *Oh, my God, it's going to go out on the street and cause a wreck.* Fortunately, the car ran into a tree and came to a stop. The only damage was a bent front bumper.

The Democratic hopefuls had one major television debate. I went. Bryce Baggett went. Wilburn Cartwright went. David Hall stayed away. He was roundly criticized for refusing to debate. His lame excuse was that he "didn't want to divide the Democratic Party." Bull! I think he didn't want to add credibility to his opponents.

Cartwright practically knocked himself out of the race as a result of his performance in this debate. The man was nearing the end of his career and obviously not as sharp as he should have been. To nearly every question, he answered, "I'll develop a program for that."

Television Speech

Shortly before the primary, I managed to cobble together enough money to buy one thirty-minute shot on a Tulsa television station for a campaign speech.

I laid out my platform. I talked about the importance of creating a constitutional highway commission.

I talked about the liquor-by-the drink-issue. I told the audience that if I had my way, I would do away with whiskey, period. I knew the problems that it caused... how many homes it broke up...how many lives it ruined. But since I couldn't stop the flow of liquor, I would rather have *controlled* liquor-by-the-drink where we could regulate it rather than having it outside the law, and hence without regulation or taxation.

I also talked about campaign finance reform. I was totally against political action committees (PACs) and out-of-state money flowing into state and local races.

That's when I told people that David Hall was a crook. Hall had so much money in his campaign that it was obscene. For example, he bought a double-decker tram in England and paid to have it transported back to Oklahoma to use in his campaign.

I talked about my opponent as anyone would do in a political speech. I said, "I have known David Hall for years, and in my opinion he has always been a crook, and he'll continue to be a crook when he gets into office.''

I knew David Hall was a crook. I lived with him for four years in the same fraternity at the University of Oklahoma. (Note: Hall was five years my junior. We were fraternity brothers as a result of my not starting college until after four years in the marines during World War II. There were four of us "old men" in the house.) During those years, I had ample opportunity to see how he operated, the way he talked, and the ideas he promulgated. Even then, I could tell he didn't have the morals of an honest man.

I didn't want Hall to have the job because I knew things would be for sale out of the governor's office if he became governor...and I said so.

Election Results

Smith Hester, chairman of the state Democratic Party, called his committee together. They sent me a letter of censure for making that statement. But since they didn't have any jurisdiction over me and couldn't drum me out of the Democratic Party, they punished me with words.

As a matter of fact, I was half-way hoping Hall would sue me for libel. But that was not likely. I knew he didn't want to get into court with me because I had the perfect defense--the truth. Truth is an absolute defense for libel. So if Hall filed suit, I could go out and take depositions, file interrogatories, and conduct an investigation. He wouldn't want that. I had conducted many investigations, and I could have proved my case.

David Hall won the primary in a walk-a-way, falling a mere 4,000 votes short of getting a clear majority, which would have avoided a runoff election. Baggett placed second, and I came in a close third. Hall won the runoff handily, then went on to win the general election in a squeaker over incumbent Republican Dewey Bartlett.

Hall's Fall

It's been said that the morals of an organization are the length and shadow of the person at the top. I witnessed an example of that tenet in Hall's administration. One of his agency heads asked me, "The governor gets a kickback on everything that's sold. How can I get in on the money?"

"You are asking the wrong man," I told him. "Don't ever ask me that question again, because if you do, I'm going to report you to the proper authorities."

As is often the case in moral matters, history was the final arbiter. The federal government proved I was right. David Hall went to prison for violations of antiracketeering statutes while he was the state's chief executive. The trial marked the first time an Oklahoma governor was convicted of criminal acts committed while in office. But it took the combined efforts of U.S. Attorney William Burkett and the FBI to do it.

Post Mortem

I spent all of the meager personal savings I had. I knew I couldn't stop the Hall juggernaught. I did it as a matter of principle.

I felt good about myself for having made the race.

§ § §

9

Donning Judicial Robes

One day in early 1973, I happened to be reading the *Oklahoma Bar Journal* when a news item caught my eye. The item referred to a vacancy for a special judge that existed on the Oklahoma County court. I decided to apply.

I went down to the courthouse to talk with Homer Smith and Carmon Harris, the two senior district judges for Oklahoma County. Both men were held in high regard as trial judges. It was important to get their blessing, inasmuch as district judges were the ones who appointed special judges.

I briefly recounted my experience and my law school grades, which were near the top of the class. I explained that despite the notoriety I got during prohibition repeal, I really was not a "whiskey raider." Rather, I was first and foremost a lawyer.

It had always been my desire, I said, to end my legal career on the bench. They had an opening, and I wanted to fill it. I wanted to start at the bottom of the judicial ladder as a special judge rather than run for election as district judge.

Smith and Harris both said, in effect, "We can't imagine somebody like you, with your credentials and experience, wanting to be a special judge."

"I want to be a trial judge with real people facing off in the courtroom. That's where the action is," I said. "I have no aspirations to be an appellate judge who sits around reading legal briefs all day every day."

Although neither of the two judges could say yes or no, they left me with the distinct feeling they were going to support my candidacy. Apparently they did, for my appointment came through a few days later.

The pay wasn't all that great. I paid more in income taxes the previous year as a trial attorney than I earned my first year as a judge.

Marryin' Joe

Right after being sworn in as a special judge, I went to my newly assigned chambers. The bailiff told me, "Judge, there's a young couple waiting here who want you to marry them."

"I don't perform marriages," I said.

They insisted that they really wanted me to be the one to marry them. My bailiff urged me to say yes.

I kept saying, "I can't marry y'all." But the bailiff and the young couple continued to stand there, all wanting me to marry them.

About that time, one of the senior district judges walked by. I called him aside so we could talk privately. "Are we really supposed to perform marriages?" I asked.

He said, "Yeah. Most people are married by judges."

I said, "Oh shit!" I never envisioned I would be marrying people. That's a holy ritual. To my way of thinking, marriage belonged in a church in front of a preacher, not a judge.

I implored him, "I don't know what to say. Do you have a book or notes or something that will help me?" He did, and he made me a copy.

Though grateful for his help, I was not satisfied with the form of the ritual he gave me. It was rigidly secular. All reference to God and anything spiritual had been stripped out. About all that remained of the ceremony was the legally-required exchange of vows.

If I was going to perform a marriage, I wanted it to be an inspiring and uplifting experience for the couple. I racked my brain for what to say. I remembered that it started out by saying, "We are gathered here today to join this man and this woman in holy matrimony." I added some words from the Preamble to the Constitution, part of the Declaration of Independence, and a quotation from Lincoln's Gettysburg Address.

I ended with, "Those that Judge Cannon and God have joined together, let no man put asunder."

Then I said, "You're married. Kiss the bride."

After I became well-established as a judge, I stopped doing marriage ceremonies unless it was for a friend whose daughter or son was getting married. Otherwise, I just wouldn't do it. Nobody had the authority to make me do it.

Judicial Duties

In Oklahoma, special judges are the lowest rung on the judicial ladder. Above them are the associate district judges and district judges.

As a special judge, I was limited in jurisdiction. I would not ordinarily try criminal felony cases. Mostly, I tried misdemeanor cases. I also held preliminary hearings in felony cases to determine whether the accused should be bound over to trial in district court.

The purpose of a preliminary hearing was to decide whether there was probable cause to believe that a crime had been committed, and whether there was probable cause to believe that this defendant committed it. The standard was not "beyond a reasonable doubt"; rather, it only required "probable cause." And if I judged there to be probable cause, I would certify the person to be tried in district court for burglary, rape, murder, or whatever the crime may be.

Small Claims

My second day on the bench found me exercising Solomon-like judgment in a small claims court case. People generally represent themselves. They don't need a lawyer.

Two aging derelicts came into court, one suing the other over a $2.00 gambling debt. These two guys lived in the homeless settlement known as "Community Camp," a shanty town of tin shacks and tents located under the Pennsylvania Avenue bridge across the Canadian River.

The petitioner was asked to state his complaint.

This rag-tag drifter pointed to his friend. "He cheated me out of two dollars in a card game." He seemed very agitated.

"You certainly have every right to come into court," I began. "That's what the court is for."

Looking at these two comical characters, I sensed that if the petitioner won his two dollars back, he would make an enemy out of the other.

Q: How many years have you two gentlemen known each other?

A: A long time, Judge."

Q: Do you play cards together every night?

A: Most nights.

Q: Do you have any other friends?

A: Not like him.

Q: Do you realize that if you win, this will probably bring your friendship to a halt?

A: I hadn't thought about that.

Q: Knowing all that, do you still want me to try this case?

A: No sir, Judge.

The two old friends walked out of the courtroom arm in arm.

Murder Trial

The Williams and Justus murder case was assigned to me while I was still a special judge. Ordinarily, special judges do not try felony cases, but there are occasions when it can happen.

The chief judge assigns cases. If there aren't enough district judges to handle all the felony cases, he'd ask the lawyers who were still waiting for their clients to go to trial, "Will anyone accept a special judge to try this case?"

Typically, a lawyer would ask, "What special judge? Who are you going to assign it to?"

The chief judge wouldn't say.

The lawyers might then say, "If you'll assign it to Judge Cannon, neither one of us will object."

He'd say, "Fine," and assign it to me.

The chief judge might as well have answered the question in the first place because if he assigned it to one of the special judges they didn't want, they could object, in which case that special judge was precluded from trying it.

That's how I got my first big murder case, the Williams and Justus case. Bill Myers was the chief judge. He asked me, "Do you feel totally and completely confident to try a criminal case?"

I said, "Well, I've prosecuted and defended a ton of them. I have no doubt but that I'm confident."

If either one of the lawyers had objected to me trying it, I couldn't have gotten the case. As it was, both the prosecuting and defending lawyers knew my experience. They knew that as a lawyer I had both prosecuted and defended God knows how many murder cases. They knew me personally, they had seen me at work on the bench, and they didn't have any objections.

I got several murder cases as a special judge because the lawyers asked for me. I got them because the lawyers in those cases knew I had tried many, many big cases as a lawyer, and they were comfortable with my ability to be a good and fair judge.

A good lawyer wants a good judge. It wasn't like the Earl Welch days when you needed one that was fixed. As a lawyer, you want a judge that is experienced and knows the law. Otherwise, you would have to prepare differently. If you had an incompetent judge like Clyde Followell, for example, who never spent a day in law school, you'd plan a different strategy than you would with an accomplished jurist like Homer Smith, Carmon Harris, Harold Theus, or Charles Owens. With them, you knew you couldn't get by with any unprofessional antics in their court.

Williams and Justus

On the evening of October 30, 1973, Cherry Lee Kennedy, 28, night clerk at Tom's Market in south Oklahoma City, was shot and killed. The police investigated and arrested two no-account hooligans named Bobby Joe Williams and Allen Clayburn Justus.

The defendants gave videotaped confessions. They testified that they were driving around south Oklahoma City in search of a place to rob. Williams was carrying a .22 caliber pistol he had recently purchased at a swap meet.

They parked in front of a Fina gas station, waiting for it to clear of customers. It didn't. A steady stream of patrons flowed in and out. After a while, they decided there were too many people around, so they moved on.

Pretty soon they found another convenience store that appeared to be a likely target. It was Tom's Market. The store was empty except for one person. They decided to kill her in order to leave no witnesses. And since they were going to kill their only witness, they decided not to wear the face masks they brought with them.

Williams entered the store while Justus remained in the car. Williams shot Ms. Kennedy in the head. The bullet passed on through and came out the other side. (.22s are notorious for doing that. The bullet is very small and will often go straight through a body, whereas a .38 will flatten out and stop.) He said the first shot went off by accident in a scuffle, but he kept shooting her until the gun ran out of bullets.

He then emptied the cash register of $33.00 and took two cartons of cigarettes. He said he and Justus split the loot.

Police found the gun. Records showed that Williams had purchased it October 2, 1973, at a swap meet for $25.00. They also recovered all of the bullets that were fired. Ray Lambert, OSBI ballistics expert, testified that the bullets that killed Cherry Kennedy came from the gun owned by Williams.

Williams and Justus were represented by the Public Defender's office. The main thing the defense tried to do was keep their clients from getting the death penalty. There really wasn't any other defense to put on.

I allowed the videotaped confessions to be shown to the jury. This was in the early days of using video in court. No issues came up with regard to that use.

The video showed them walking into the room, being advised

of their rights, and signing a waiver. Those two guys were sitting there acting like they were having a big time. They were stars of the show.

Bobby Joe Williams and Allen Clayburn Justus were convicted and given the death penalty.

Our use of video was brought up on appeal. The Court of Criminal Appeals pointed out in its opinion that as long as someone testified that it was done, done right, nothing was edited out of it, and it matched their written confession exactly, the issue of videotape was moot.

The U.S. Supreme Court later ruled the Oklahoma death penalty statute unconstitutional, and the sentences of Williams and Justus were reduced to life imprisonment. Oklahoma, at that time, did not have a penalty of life without the possibility of parole.

Snitches. The interesting thing about this case is that the district attorney probably would have had a helluva time convicting them if it weren't for the confessions. That's the only real evidence they had except for the .22 pistol. The gun was corroborating evidence for the confessions.

Williams and Justus were probably fingered by snitches. That's the way police catch most criminals. Oklahoma City has a really fine bunch of detectives. They've got snitches everywhere, especially in whorehouses.

For some reason or another, when a major crime is committed, the crook feels an urge to tell someone about it. Most of the time, the person they tell is a prostitute. Since prostitutes are usually in trouble with the law themselves, the detective will promise to go to bat for them with the DA whenever they're picked up in exchange for them passing on information to him.

Most of the time when a snitch passes information to a detective, it's something that relates to corroborating evidence.

Criminal Mind. Criminals can't see the overall picture. They don't see the tie-ins that good detectives and district attorneys know. That is, how can you tie this bit of information into something that's really important to show that what is described is really true?

They don't understand that process. They don't think about it. And most of them don't think they'll ever get caught.

Broken Zipper

Thank God for judicial robes.

During a recess in the middle of a jury trial one day, I took advantage of the opportunity to go to the restroom. I had a minor catastrophe. The zipper on my pants broke. That put me in a quandary. It was not practical to go home for a change of clothes because I lived in Edmond, some twenty miles away. Meanwhile, lawyers and jurors were waiting impatiently for me to resume the trial.

I phoned Connelly's mens store in downtown Oklahoma City. Joe Connelly, a friend of mine, answered the phone. I told Joe what had happened. He said, "Send them over, and I'll have my tailor fix them."

I sent Abram Ross, my bailiff, down to the store with my pants. Then I went back to the bench with just my robe and long black socks hiding the fact that I wasn't wearing any trousers. I had to move very carefully.

Everything went fine until we had to take another recess. Four lawyers came into my chambers to get me to sign some legal papers. They became curious as to why I was sitting so primly behind my desk and wearing my robe.

"Judge, it is a very warm day," one of them said. "Why are you sitting here in your chambers with your robe on?"

"Because I don't have any pants on."

"Yeah, sure, Judge." They didn't believe me.

"Here, see for yourself." I stood up, raised my robe, and showed them my long, skinny legs with nothing on but shorts and black socks. "Talk about getting caught with your pants down," I wisecracked.

Happily for my sense of propriety, Abram came back at that moment with my newly-repaired pants. I put them on and went back into the courtroom. The jury was none the wiser.

Judge's Disease

After I had been on the bench several months, I began to exhibit what some people call "the judge's disease." That happens when one gets so puffed up with self importance that he tries to rule everything at home as well as in the courtroom.

Out of the mouths of babes comes wisdom. One evening my family was seated around the table at dinner. This involved my wife, Caroline; Scott, our son; and our two daughters, Dana and Toni. Apparently, I got to acting pretty bossy, because ten-year-old Toni, the youngest, piped up and said, "Daddy, you are not the judge here at home!"

District Judge

I decided to run for district judge in 1974 when a vacancy opened up on the district court. Judge Robert Blinn was rumored to be thinking about retirement.

District judges were elected rather than appointed. The law said that if a special judge wished to run against an incumbent district judge, he would have to resign first.

One of my fellow special judges, George Pendell, said that he was going to run whether Blinn retired or not. That, of course, meant that he was prepared to resign.

I said I wouldn't run if Judge Blinn was going to run for reelection. I went down to talk with the judge and explain the situation. "George Pendell says he's going to run whether you run or not," I said, "but I'm not going to run if you're going to run."

Blinn replied, "I'm not making it public yet, and I don't want you to, but I am telling you because you had the courtesy to come down and talk to me about it. I'm not going to run. So you can get prepared to run if you want to."

Pendell and I faced off against each other in the general election. He lost; and in January 1975 I moved up to the district court.

§ § §

10

Judging Murders

Someone asked me one time why my name appeared in the newspapers so often. My answer? "I wasn't seeking headlines; the headlines found me."

Let's face it, the news media thrives on the sensational. Murder makes news. There is nothing they like more than a lurid murder trial. Couple this with the fact that I got more murder cases than any other judge down at the courthouse, and you have a recipe for generating a lot of headlines.

During my last term on the bench, I tried sixty-one murder cases without a reversal. (In one, the sentencing stage was reversed but not the conviction.) I mentioned that fact to former District Judge Bill Burkett over lunch at the Oklahoma City Golf and Country Club. "That's an amazing record!" he exclaimed.

Bob Ravitz, head of Oklahoma County's public defender's office, was another fan. He used to try to have his cases assigned to my court, openly telling colleagues, "Joe Cannon knows more about how to try a murder case than anybody else in the courthouse."

Michael Wayne Green

My first murder case after being elected associate district judge, but not yet having taken office, was that of Michael Wayne Green. The trial took place November 12-14, 1974.

The previous April 16, police got a call at 2:30 a.m. about a disturbance at the Tip Toe Inn, a ratty, old bar at Harrison and Walnut Avenues in Oklahoma City. Officers James D. Chamblin and John C. Campbell responded to the call.

Green was in a booth with three other people. He appeared drunk. The officers arrested him on a charge of public drunkenness and walked him out to the police car. They didn't put handcuffs on him because that is seldom necessary with ordinary drunks. Green repeatedly asked why he was being arrested but was so drunk he couldn't comprehend what the officers were telling him.

Suddenly, Green pulled a pistol out of his pocket and fired at both officers. Chamblin fell to the ground, and Green shot him a second time. Campbell, though wounded, scrambled around to the opposite side of the police car where he laid in wait for Green to come around the car after him. Instead, Green fired a couple more shots underneath the car, wounding Campbell a second time, then took off running towards an alley.

It was now Campbell's turn. He fired four shots at the fleeing felon.

Other police officers arrived on the scene in response to a call that a police officer had been shot. Officer Campbell gave them a description of the man who had shot them and pointed where to look. They found Green in a dead-end alley with a .38 caliber revolver at his side. The officers shot when he turned his gun on them, severely wounding Green in the chest.

The police took Green by ambulance down to Mercy Hospital, where the doctors saved his life.

It turned out that Green was an escapee from a North Carolina prison. Perhaps that explains why he tried to shoot his way out of a simple drunkenness arrest. He knew if they took him to jail, they'd run a tracer on him, and he would end up back in the North Carolina prison.

Michael Wayne Green was a pathetic-looking creature when he appeared in my court on November 12. Wheeled into the courtroom in a wheelchair, he was small, slight of build, mustachioed, and visibly suffering the after-effects of his gunshot wounds.

Green was represented by assistant public defender T. Hurley Jordan. Jordan sought to postpone the trial because of Green's physical condition.

The prosecuting attorney was assistant DA Duane Miller. He objected.

I put in a telephone call to Dr. Joe Dan Metcalf, Green's attending physician, with both attorneys on the line. Dr. Metcalf said Green was able to attend trial.

The prosecution put on only five witnesses. Officer Campbell's testimony was by far the most dramatic. The prosecutor led him through the story, second by second, of the events that occurred on the morning of April 16.

"Who shot your partner?" the prosecutor asked.

Campbell pointed with his whole arm in a forceful gesture, his voice charged with emotion. "He did! That man right over there, Michael Wayne Green, shot my partner."

With that, the prosecution rested. It was now time for the defense to put on its case.

Green's attorney offered no defense. Instead, he rested the case immediately after the state closed.

The jury deliberated little more than thirty minutes before finding Green guilty of murder in the first degree. The charge carried an automatic death penalty.

The surest way to get the death penalty in Oklahoma was to kill a policeman. Killing a police officer in the line of duty is classified as an aggravating circumstance, and it gives the jury the right to give the death sentence.

Epilogue. An interesting coincidence occurred some twenty years later. I had retired from the judgeship and moved to Florida where Caroline and I lived on a boat based in Destin.

In 1995, civil defense officials reported that Hurricane Opal was headed directly toward our town, and they ordered us to evacuate the area. We packed as many belongings as we could into the car and drove six hours through hurricane winds and rain to Clanton, Alabama, where we had friends who were willing to take us in.

We weren't the only ones. Several people of various ages had taken refuge there also. Among them was a friend of our hosts' son, a young man in his early twenties. We all gathered in the large living room. As we got acquainted with each other, it came out that I was a retired judge from Oklahoma City.

"Do you know anything about a man named Michael Wayne Green who killed a police officer?" the young man asked.

"Yes, I was the judge in that case," I told him.

"That police officer was my father," he said softly. He said he was eighteen months old when his father died. His mother moved out of state and remarried; and because of the pain involved she never told him about his birth father. He asked me what I could tell him about the death of his father and the status of his father's killer.

We went off to a secluded area, and he and I talked privately for a couple hours. He had many questions. I answered each question as best I could, which seemed to provide some closure to him regarding the facts and circumstances of his father's death. I told him that Michael Wayne Green was still on death row in Oklahoma and going through a seemingly endless appeal process.

The next day, after the storm had passed and we were driving back to Florida, I got to wondering. What were the odds that people evacuating from a hurricane to a place they had never been before and meeting people they had never seen before, would result in a young man and a retired judge coming together regarding a murder that took place twenty years earlier?

To my way of thinking, this was an amazing coincidence.

Wishon and Williams

On the evening of January 12, 1974, two seventeen-year-old boys, Frederick Hamilton Wishon and Sammy Duane Williams, were "tripping" on LSD at Williams' home in Edmond, Oklahoma.

They had recently seen the movie, *Papillon,* a Steve McQueen thriller about a real-life escape from the French penal colony of Devil's Island. One gory scene showed a man's throat being slashed from ear to ear.

That image played on Wishon's mind. "I'm going to kill Tommy Mantooth," he told Williams.

Tommy Lee Mantooth was thirteen. Wishon claimed that Mantooth had raped his girlfriend a year earlier.

The two drove around the familiar haunts of Edmond, Oklahoma, looking for Mantooth. They found him at the Arcadia Amusement Center. They told Mantooth they had some marijuana stashed in a vacant lot, and they persuaded him to go with them to smoke some. They got in Wishon's car and drove around Edmond a while before going to a vacant lot in the Meadowlark addition.

While Mantooth was looking for buried marijuana, Wishon stepped up behind him and slashed his throat. Both Wishon and Williams stood and watched Mantooth grab his throat and fall down, kicking and clawing at the ground. Then they went back to the car.

Williams said, "You'd better go back and see that he's really dead, because if he isn't you'll be in a lot of trouble." Wishon returned to the murder scene and cut Mantooth's throat some more.

Mantooth was nearly decapitated in the knifing. The medical examiner reported that "functionally speaking, only one major artery from his body to the top of his head was left intact."

Following the slaying, the boys returned to their homes. They lived next door to each other. Williams sat up all night at the back door watching for Wishon, afraid of what Wishon might do. Come morning, he went to the Edmond Police Department to report the killing, and he led officers to Mantooth's body.

The trial of Wishon and Williams began December 11, 1974. The two were tried together. Both boys, now eighteen, were certified as adults.

The trial itself was pretty much cut and dried. The Edmond police had confessions from both boys, although Wishon sought to disclaim his. Williams testified freely on the stand. "I didn't believe him," he said when Wishon told him he was going to kill Tommy Mantooth.

The jury deliberated an hour and forty minutes. The verdict for Wishon was guilty of murder in the first degree. It carried the death penalty. (Note: When Wishon went back and slashed the victim again to make sure he was dead, that indicated a clear intent to kill.)

Somewhat surprisingly, Williams was acquitted. I had thought Williams to be an accessory to murder, but the jury didn't see it that way. Under Oklahoma law, an accessory to murder is as guilty as the trigger man. For example, if you and I go down to a bank with a scheme to rob it, and I shoot one of the tellers, both of us could be convicted of murder one, even though you didn't have a gun.

On the other hand, if the jury had found him guilty, I probably wouldn't have let the death penalty stand. Williams really didn't do anything except when they got back in the car and he told Wishon to make sure Mantooth was dead.

Upon hearing the verdict, Wishon's mother ran from the courtroom shouting, "It isn't fair! It just isn't fair!" I sent a deputy to make sure she was OK.

John Benjamin Kennedy, Jr.

The first time that bite marks were used in Oklahoma to identify a criminal occurred in a 1978 murder trial I conducted.

A fellow named John Benjamin Kennedy, Jr., rented a room at King's Inn, a cheap motel at 10th and Robinson in Oklahoma City. He called for and got a prostitute, fifteen-year-old Yvonne Jolene McFaddin. Then he killed her. Cause of death was strangulation.

God only knows what kind of kinky sex he demanded, because he nearly bit off one of her breasts. She must have bled quite a bit for blood was spattered all over the place.

The police arrested Kennedy and he was bound over for trial in my court. They had plenty of evidence. The motel clerk testified he rented this guy the room, and he identified him in court as the one that was in the room. They had Kennedy's fingerprints all over the place; and blood on his clothes matched that of the victim. (There was no DNA testing in those days.)

The principal issue at trial was the use of expert witness testimony to compare bite marks on the woman's body with the tooth pattern of the defendant. In order to make such a comparison, the prosecution needed a plaster cast of Kennedy's teeth. He refused to let them make one. The prosecution asked me for a court order to compel the defendant to let the expert make a plaster cast. Kennedy's attorney fought it as an invasion of privacy and an abuse of the Fourth Amendment of the U.S. Constitution protection against unreasonable search and seizure.

I issued the order. I compared it to fingerprints; you can't refuse to allow the police to fingerprint you even though it may be giving evidence against yourself, in a way.

The prosecution called two expert witnesses, Dr. Richard Thomas Glass and Dr. Edward E. Andrews, both of the University of Oklahoma College of Dentistry and Medicine. They were experts on oral pathology, prosthodontics, and maxillofacial prosthetics.

The defense fought tooth and nail against their qualifications as expert witnesses. I ruled that they were qualified to testify in this matter. In making this ruling I laid down the law on the qualifications for an expert.

Dr. Andrews testified that it was "within reasonable medical probability" that Kennedy caused the bite marks on the woman's body.

The defense put on its own expert. Dr. James D. Woodward of the Oral Roberts' dental school said Kennedy's abscessed teeth would not have permitted him to make such bites because of the pain it would cause him. The jury didn't buy it.

Kennedy was found guilty of murder in the first degree and sentenced to life imprisonment. (Note: The U.S. Supreme Court had ruled Oklahoma's death penalty statute unconstitutional in 1976, and the state had not yet adopted a sentence of life without the possibility of parole.)

Kennedy's conviction made its way to Oklahoma's Court of Criminal Appeals. The appellate court affirmed my rulings. In ruling this way, the court said I "made a fair and informed decision regarding qualifying these witnesses as experts."

This ruling made Oklahoma the ninth state to recognize bite marks as evidence.

Federal Bench

All of my life I had wanted to retire on a boat and live in Florida. I knew that on a district judge's salary I'd never accumulate enough money to do that. So in February 1978 when a federal judgeship opened up in Tampa, Florida, I applied. It paid nearly twice as much as Oklahoma and had better benefits and a lighter caseload. I got the job.

Before leaving town, however, there was one little thing I wanted to take care of. That was to pay tribute to a gentleman named Abram Ross.

Long before I ascended to the bench, I told myself that if I ever became a judge I wanted Abram Ross to be my bailiff. Abram was a courtly, soft-spoken, silver-haired black man of dignity who, at age sixty-four, embarked on a new career--that of court bailiff. To the best of my knowledge, he was the first black man ever to occupy that post in Oklahoma.

He was well-known in the community from his many years as a radio disk jockey, newscaster, and television personality. His daily radio program on an Oklahoma City station, called "Negroes in the News," attracted a wide following. During the disastrous Watts riots in 1965, Abram was invited by the Los Angeles City Council to go there as an ambassador of good will. His daily newscasts from the riot scene were broadcast on several Los Angeles-area stations and in Oklahoma City.

Abram became an instant hit among the courthouse crowd. He was already familiar with courtroom procedures because that's where he got a lot of the news he reported. To strangers for whom this might be their first visit to the courthouse, he was always kind and helpful.

People loved the way he opened court: "All rise, please. The District Court of Oklahoma County is now in session...the Honorable Joe Cannon presiding." Time and again, he came tantalizingly close to saying, "and here comes da Judge." I had to remind him that it would not be good courtroom decorum to say that.

My fellow judges threw a going-away party for me on my last day on the bench. I spread the word that I was going to let Abram open court for my final session the way he always wanted to. It would be at 2:00 p.m. on a motion docket.

By two o'clock that afternoon the courtroom was full to overflowing. Not even standing room. It seemed like every lawyer in town was there.

They were not disappointed. Abram intoned, "Hear ye. Hear ye. The District Court of Oklahoma County is now in session with the Honorable Joe Cannon presiding." He paused, looked around the room, smiled, then uttered the words everyone came to hear: "Everybody rise, 'cause here comes da Judge."

I've never been so disappointed in my life as I was with the Florida federal judgeship. I primarily conducted Social Security hearings where all I did was shuffle papers all day. There was nothing to it. No criminal law. No challenge. I could do that work in my sleep. It got so bad I hated to go to work in the morning.

Caroline had stayed behind to sell our house. It took about four months for her to wind up our affairs in Oklahoma City, then she came down to join me. She was in Florida about two weeks when I announced, "We're moving home."

Homer Smith was the presiding judge of the district court in Oklahoma City. I called Homer. "I hear you have a special judgeship open. If I come back home, can I have it?"

"As far as I'm concerned, you can. I'll see to it that you do get it."

So I started over at the bottom of the ladder.

Rita Silk Nauni

Presiding Judge Jack Parr must have had retribution in mind when he assigned the Rita Silk Nauni murder case to me. He said the trial was apt to be a three-ring circus, and he needed someone who could give Nauni a fair trial but keep control of the courtroom.

Rita Silk Nauni, 31, was a Standing Rock Sioux Indian who flew into Oklahoma City on September 19, 1979, on her way to Fort Sill to see her first husband, the father of her son. She was currently married to a Black Muslim member of a Los Angeles motorcycle gang.

Apparently, Nauni decided to hitchhike to Lawton, Oklahoma, where Fort Sill was located. Two airport police officers, Garland Garrison and Teresa Wells, spotted her walking along Airport Road, staggering and acting very peculiar. They thought she was drunk. They stopped to investigate. It turned out she was on dope.

Nauni and the female officer got into a scuffle. Nauni managed to grab Wells' gun and shoot both Wells and her partner. Garrison died at the scene and Wells was severely wounded. Nauni then took off in the police car.

An "officer down" call went out, and a whole slew of cop cars joined the high speed chase. Nauni kept shooting at police cars as long as she had bullets in the gun. Eventually, she lost control of the car and crashed into a barrier. She was arrested for the murder of a police officer and taken to the Oklahoma County jail.

Jack Parr was only half right. This wasn't a three-ring circus; it had the makings of a ten-ring circus.

Somehow, the Indian activists had adopted Rita Silk Nauni and transformed her into a figurehead, a symbol, a martyr for their cause. The U.S. Government, for reasons I know not, sent buses to Wounded Knee, South Dakota, to bring Indians to Oklahoma City for the trial. Lending a festive atmosphere was Hollywood celebrity Will Sampson, who played "Big Chief" in the movie *One Flew Over the Cuckoo's Nest*. He came to draw attention to a pre-trial rally.

The Indians held a big rally around the courthouse the night before the trial began. They did war dances and everything all night long. I went out there that evening before they started, and I told them, "You can march around the courthouse, hold up signs, or do whatever you want to do under the First Amendment to the Constitution. But you can't pitch tepees or start bonfires."

The participants were attired in colorful Indian garb, wore beautiful Indian jewelry, and sported hats with beaded bands. They kept up an all-night vigil of beating the drums, dancing, and singing Indian songs on the courthouse lawn. It was a peaceful demonstration and for them, meaningful.

A news reporter asked me how a white judge could give Rita a fair trial. I told him, "We don't try Indians, we try people." Besides, I added, "almost everyone in Oklahoma has a little Indian blood."

Had he bothered to follow up on his own question, I would have told him that not only was I part Indian myself, but my wife was a great-great-granddaughter of a Cherokee chief. Her mother graduated from Bacone Indian College.

I never knew what to expect when I walked into the courtroom each day. On the first three days of the trial, the activists made three different types of entrance.

The first day, they wouldn't stand up. I lectured them, "You aren't standing up for me, because you can look up here and see that when the bailiff is opening court, I'm standing up too. We don't sit down until he opens the court and says the things he says. It's not in respect for me individually, it's in respect for the court and the State of Oklahoma."

Twenty or more deputy sheriffs patrolled the courtroom and hallways because I had no idea what this crowd of sixty or seventy Indians was going to do. After all, Wounded Knee is where they had that shootout with U.S. marshals. Metal detectors screened people for weapons as they entered courtroom. I needed enough armed deputies on hand to quell a riot, if one should break out.

I told them, "I'm going to go back into my chambers, and I'm going to have the bailiff open court again. The ones that don't

stand up are in contempt, and I'll have a deputy escort them
straight to jail.''

I came back, the bailiff opened court again, and every one of
them stood up.

I ran into a similar problem the second day. They all stood up,
all right, but they all had their hats on. They were wearing those
flat-top, Indian-style hats with wide brims. So I went through the
same process again. ''You can't wear your hats in the courtroom.
When the bailiff opens court and I walk in, you've got to take
your hats off.'' I told the deputies, ''The ones that don't take their
hats off, take them straight to jail.''

The third day, the demonstrators got there early so as to get
seats as close as possible to the jury box. This time, they were
puffing ritual pipes and blowing and fanning the smoke towards
the jury box. Somehow, in some magical fashion, the smoke was
supposed to influence the jurors in a positive way.

I told them, ''You can't do that either. We're not going to have
any Indian *cungee* in this room during this trial.'' By this time the
routine was familiar--I went back out, came back in, and the pipes
were gone from sight.

I think it surprised them that I knew what the word *cungee*
meant.

Rita Silk Nauni was represented by Doug Parr, a lawyer who
worked for an Indian legal services agency. Although not Indian
himself, he was well-respected in the Indian community.

Parr was assisted by Barry Benefield, a white man who had
adopted Indian ways. Barry was the son of a prominent Oklahoma
lawyer and political powerhouse. Benefield dressed in cast-off
clothes, wore his hair in a braided ponytail, and looked as if he'd
slept the night in the back of a car.

The prosecutor was Stanley P. Pierce, 49, an assistant district
attorney for Oklahoma County. His boss, Andy Coats, had
recently resigned as DA to run for the U.S. Senate and Pierce was
a candidate for the position.

The trial went on for two weeks. It was a spirited fight between the prosecution and the defense. Doug Parr did a good job in this trial, made a good argument, and conducted good cross-examination. He tried as good a case as he had facts to try.

One day, looking across the courtroom, I saw something that appeared to be a violation of the attorneys' dress code. The problem was with Barry Benefield. The seam in his pants was split all the way from his crotch to the belt line, and he wasn't wearing any underwear. His bare butt showed whenever he moved.

I stopped the trial, sent the jury out, and asked all the lawyers to come into my chambers. I said, "Mr. Benefield, you are not dressed properly to appear in court."

He didn't seem at all embarrassed.

Since the time was getting near the noon break, I announced that the lunch hour would start a little early this day. I instructed Barry, "Before you can come back into this courtroom as a lawyer, you've got to get some proper clothes."

Barry returned from lunch with some good pants on.

At the end of the trial, the jury found Rita Silk Nauni guilty of the murder of a police officer. She was sentenced to 150 years imprisonment.

Following the trial, the defense lawyers filed a motion to set aside the jury verdict and give her a new trial. Such motions are introduced in every criminal case before they can file an appeal to the Court of Criminal Appeals. A hearing on this motion is held before the judge who tried the case.

The defense brought in famed Chicago lawyer William Kunstler to argue the motion. He achieved notoriety in the 1970 circus-like trial of the infamous "Chicago Seven," in which he nearly drove a federal judge crazy with his courtroom antics.

On my way to the office that morning, I heard Kunstler being interviewed on radio. He had just landed at the airport. He told the reporter that he had come down here to straighten out these hick judges who didn't know any law. He said he was going to go down to the courthouse and straighten me out.

I couldn't believe he was that arrogant.

Doug Parr had gotten my friend, attorney James W. "Bill" Berry to make a motion that Kunstler be permitted to appear in this court and argue this case. (Note: Oklahoma law requires that a member of the Oklahoma Bar must make the motion to permit an out-of-state lawyer who's not a member of the Oklahoma Bar to appear in this court and argue this one case.)

When Bill finished making the motion, I said, "No."

It took him totally by surprise.

I said, "No, Mr. Kunstler is not welcome in this court. I know who Mr. Kunstler is, and he will not be permitted to appear in this court."

Kunstler proceeded to go over and sit down at the counsel table beside Doug Parr. I said, "Mr. Kunstler, you are not permitted to be on this side of the bar. You'll have to sit back in the audience if you wish to stay."

He got up, and as he was walking out, he said, "You are an un-American judge, and this is an un-American court."

I told one of the deputies, "Bring that man back up here in front of the bench."

The deputy took him by the arm and brought him back up to the bench. I said, "I think I know what you said. Did I hear you correctly, did you say I was an un-American judge and this was an un-American court?"

He said, "Yes sir, I did."

"I am holding you in contempt of court. I am holding a hearing at two o'clock this afternoon. You can either hire yourself a lawyer or represent yourself at the hearing to show what your punishment shall be, and you may attempt to explain why you should not be held in contempt of court."

I had Sheriff J.D. Sharp himself take him to jail. I told Sharp, "Sheriff, I want you personally to take him to jail, I want him dressed out as a prisoner, and I want him put in a cell. He's not to sit out in the lobby."

At two o'clock, I brought Kunstler back into court. He was elegantly attired in orange jail coveralls. He said he was sorry, that he really didn't mean it. He told me two or three times that he was sorry.

I said, "Well, I think you are really in contempt of court, but there will be no punishment."

He left, boarded an airplane, and went back to Chicago. Before the afternoon was over, I got a telegram. It read, "When I told you I was sorry, I didn't mean it. Signed. William Kuntsler."

There wasn't anything I could do to him in Chicago. That was out of my jurisdiction.

Several months later, a local attorney reported having heard Kunstler say, "As long as Cannon is on the bench, I am not going to show myself in the state of Oklahoma."

Epilogue. A dozen or so years later, my wife and I journeyed back for a visit to Oklahoma City from our retirement home in Florida. I stopped at a traffic light in the southern part of town.

As I was waiting for the light to change, a woman's voice spoke to me from the car on my left. "Hello, Judge."

I looked over. It was Rita Silk Nauni. "Hello, Rita," I said. "I see you are out on parole."

"Yes, sir," she replied.

"It must feel pretty good to be free for awhile."

"Yes, sir. It sure does."

The light turned green. "Good luck, Judge," she said.

"Good luck to you, Rita."

We both drove off, never to cross paths again.

Murder Law Handbook

Oklahoma's Court of Criminal Appeals called a statewide conference of all district judges when the U.S. Supreme Court authorized the states to begin having the death penalty again. The seminar was held in the courtroom of the Court of Criminal Appeals. Every district judge was mandated to be there.

I had written a handbook on murder laws. Tom Brett, chief justice of the Court of Criminal Appeals, read my little book.

Brett called me aside when I checked in at the registration desk. "You don't know it yet, Joe, but you're going to teach this seminar.''

That caught me completely by surprise. I protested that I hadn't had time to prepare. But Brett insisted, ''We've got your book, and we think you're exactly right.''

I went ahead and made a presentation. I was totally confident in what I was doing. I felt I knew more about our murder laws than any judge in the state of Oklahoma. I had probably tried more murder cases than any judge in the state of Oklahoma. I generally knew what a lawyer was going to object to before he objected, and I knew how I was going to rule because I'd ruled on that issue a hundred times before.

When I finished, I told the judges, ''When you run into a problem on a murder case, call me. My bailiff has instructions that if a judge calls me, he should get me off the bench--even if I'm in a trial--and I'll be glad to answer your question.''

You can't believe how many of them took my offer and called me from all over the state.

Glen Burton Ake

Glen Burton Ake was one mean son of a bitch. He tried to kill the judge who tried him for the October 1979 murders of the Rev. Richard Douglass and his wife, Marilyn, in their Okarche, Oklahoma, home. Floyd Martin of El Reno was the trial judge whom Ake tried to kill. Ake was given the death penalty.

The U.S. Supreme Court overturned Ake's conviction in 1985, and in the process they wrote new law. They said he should have been granted his request for a court-paid psychiatrist.

When Ake's second trial came along, Judge Martin was off the bench, his successor had to disqualify himself, and I was appointed to try the case in Canadian County.

Facts. Glen Burton Ake and Steven Keith Hatch worked as roughnecks in various oil fields around Canadian County. They decided to move out west but didn't have any money. So they stole a car from the rig site, did a little target practice with a .357 magnum pistol, then began looking for a wealthy homeowner to rob.

They chose the residence of the Rev. Richard Douglass. It was an affluent-looking country home just outside the town of Okarche. Douglass was pastor of Putnam City Baptist Church, a suburb of Oklahoma City.

Ake and Hatch used the pretext of having car trouble and needing to use the telephone. Almost any Christian family would offer help. The Douglasses were no exception. After all, Richard was a Baptist preacher. He was a trusting soul who had no idea somebody was going to come out there and do harm to his family.

The two hoodlums, ages 23 and 25, held the family at gunpoint while they hog-tied and gagged them. They left them lying on the living room floor except for the daughter, twelve-year-old Leslie. They made her lead them around the house looking for valuables. The only money she could find was her piggy bank. They broke it open and took the few dollars that were in it.

They tried to rape her. She fought and screamed, but they were unable to make penetration. Hell, she wasn't but twelve years old at the time. They even used shaving cream as a lubricant, and still they couldn't. She was just too little, just a child.

They gave up on rape, brought her into the living room with the rest of the family, tied her up, and put tape over her mouth.

Ake sent Hatch back out to the car. That's when he shot everybody. The girl was shot three times, the father twice, and the boy and the mother once. He thought he had killed them all.

If it hadn't been for the courage of sixteen-year-old Brooks Douglass, all probably would have died. He finally worked himself loose from the cord that bound him. He knew both his mother and father were dead--he had watched them die. His sister, though badly disfigured, was still moaning.

Wounded as he was, Brooks untied his sister, put her in the car, and drove to the home of Dr. Jack Berry, their family doctor, who lived two miles away. Fortunately, the doctor was home. He immediately applied emergency treatment that saved their lives.

Meanwhile, Ake and Hatch fled to Texas where they killed two more people in a similar manner. They were captured five weeks

later while committing a robbery in northwest Colorado and were
returned to Oklahoma for trial.

First trial. Ake and Hatch were brought before Judge Floyd
Martin in El Reno, county seat of Canadian County. Ake asked
for a jury trial. Hatch waived a jury trial in favor of a trial before
the judge. Apparently, he figured that since Judge Martin was also
a part-time preacher, he would be less inclined than a jury to
assign the death penalty--particularly since Hatch was not the
shooter.

Ake and Hatch were tried separately. Ake pleaded insanity. It
didn't work. The jury convicted him in July 1980 of first degree
murder and sentenced him to death.

The conviction was upheld in the Oklahoma Court of Criminal
Appeals but overturned by the U.S. Supreme Court. The justices
said that Judge Martin should have appointed a psychiatrist to aid
Ake in his defense. This was new law. It had never been applied
before. From that time forward, if an indigent defendant pleads
insanity in a death penalty case, it is the duty of the trial judge to
appoint a psychiatrist to help him with his defense.

When the case came back to Canadian County, there had been a
change in judges. District Judge Stan C. Chatman now occupied
the bench. However, he had to disqualify himself because
previously, as assistant district attorney, he had helped investigate
the case.

That's how I got named to retry Glen Burton Ake for murder.

Second trial. The new trial was set to begin February 3, 1986. I
appointed Dr. Hans von Brauchitsch, head of the department of
adult psychiatry at the University of Oklahoma College of
Medicine. Everybody called him "Dr. von B" because nobody
could pronounce his last name.

I told him I harbored a skeptical attitude toward so-called
"expert" testimony from psychiatrists. I didn't have a problem
with expert witnesses such as MDs, metallurgists, geologists, and
the like where objective standards can be applied. But a lawyer

can always find a psychiatrist who will testify either way, that a guy is crazy or he's not crazy, whichever side the lawyer chooses. All he has to do is pay the psychiatrist his fee.

Dr. von B invited me to come out to the medical school and talk to his students. I said, "You really don't want me to come out there because it's not going to be very favorable towards your profession. I don't think you guys know what you're talking about." But he asked me to come anyway. I did, and we had a great time with the students.

Protective measures. Irven Box was appointed to defend Ake. None of the lawyers in El Reno wanted to have anything to do with him. Box and his assistant counsel came to me one day and said they were really worried about what might happen at the trial. They said he was so mean and so strong that he could break somebody's neck with just one twist.

During his 1980 trial in Judge Martin's court, Ake jumped up from the counsel table and tried to climb up on the bench and kill Judge Martin. He was a psychopath. Ake was so strong he picked up one deputy, lifted him clear above his head, and slammed him to the floor. It took three deputies to restrain him. He told them later that he intended to kill the judge if he could have gotten up there.

"What do you think we ought to do?" I asked Box. "We've got to figure out some way to make sure he's restrained."

Box and his assistant thought Ake might jump up and kill someone in the courtroom, and they were afraid it might be one of them. They said Ake was capable of committing a violent act solely to convince the jury he was crazy and didn't know the difference between right and wrong, and therefore get off with life instead of death.

I held a hearing in my chambers outside the presence of the jury. Defense counsel put into the record with a court reporter present that they were afraid of what Ake might do.

I said, "Well, I can't shackle him in front of a brand-new jury, so I've got to figure out some way to do it."

That's when I came up with the idea of a curtain. I bounced it off them. "Why don't we have the county buy a cloth that will form a skirt around the table clear to the floor, and put it on both the state's and the defense's tables so that the jury doesn't wonder why Ake has one and the district attorney doesn't?"

I always had him brought in first and seated in his chair with his feet covered by the skirt, then brought the jury in. They never saw that he was shackled.

In his appeal, Ake's attorney cited the fact that he was shackled, but the Court of Criminal Appeals threw that out because the jury was never aware of that fact.

We had his feet together so he couldn't jump up and run. His hands were free, of course, and he could put them up on top of the table just like everybody else.

He behaved himself in my court. Never made an outcry, never said a word.

One reason why he behaved was the presence of a deputy sheriff in the courtroom who was one tough hombre. The deputy suggested that if he stood behind Ake and put his foot on the back rung of the chair, Ake couldn't try to get up without him knowing it. And that's just what the deputy did.

Ake was present at this proceeding and was hearing all that was being said. I turned to him, "Now, Mr. Ake, if you try to get up from that chair, even though you're shackled, I have instructed that deputy sheriff to shoot you in the back of the head. If you move that chair backwards even one inch, he's going to shoot you without asking. You're going to die right then and there. Do you understand?"

He said, "Yes sir, I do."

Throughout the trial he sat with his head bowed, trying to act crazy. Never opened his mouth. Never made a sound.

Every recess, we'd take the jury out first, then take Ake out...back to the county jail for lunch, etc. The main reason I shackled him was that his own lawyers were afraid he might jump up and kill one of them.

Prosecution. The prosecuting attorney was Cathy Stocker of Enid, Oklahoma. Her district covered five counties, including Canadian County where the trial was being held. Now in her mid thirties, she had been district attorney since 1982.

Brooks and Leslie Douglass were both called to testify. It was painful for them to relive those events. They identified Glen Burton Ake as the gunman who killed their parents and left them for dead nearly seven years earlier.

Brooks Douglass, now 22, told the jury, "Ake said, 'Well, I don't want to shoot you, but....' And I heard a shot go off and felt a bullet hit me in the back."

He described how he crawled to his parents after the assailants left, only to watch them die.

Leslie, now 19 and a student at the University of Central Oklahoma, said the family believed Ake when he approached the house alone, asking for assistance. However, he left on the pretext of getting a telephone number from his car, and then returned armed with a pistol and with Hatch, who carried a shotgun. While the other family members were bound face down in the living room, Ake forced her to accompany him around the house to show him "secret hiding places" in her bedroom.

Dr. Jack Berry, the family physician to whom the Douglass children drove for medical aid, also testified for the prosecution.

Stocker played tapes from the first trial in 1980 in which Ake admitted firing the fatal shots. The defense tried to keep Ake's confession out of the trial, but I ruled that he voluntarily made the taped statement for former Canadian County Sheriff D.L. Stedman.

Ake told of driving with Steven Keith Hatch to the Douglass home October 15, 1979, with the intent of robbing the family. He said he told Hatch to go to the borrowed car they had waiting outside. He said he looked at the family as they lay on the living room floor, "and I stands by the end of the couch and I unloaded the .357 magnum loaded with .38 wadcutters." He said he left after firing the sixth shot.

Defense. Irven Box had a reputation for being flamboyant, but he didn't exhibit any of that flamboyance in this trial. Except for his tennis shoes, that is. Box always wore tennis shoes. That was his trademark. I guess I could have said that he wasn't properly attired to try a case in district court. But I didn't. It wasn't material.

Box conducted a straightforward and well-reasoned argument. But he didn't have much to work with.

The principal defense he put on was an insanity plea. He wasn't saying Ake didn't do it; rather, he was saying Ake was crazy at the time and wasn't responsible for what he was doing. That's why we had to appoint him a psychiatrist. This new precedent was now the law of the land, so I appointed the best psychiatrist we could find. That turned out to be Dr. von Brauchitsch.

von Brauchitsch was the only defense witness. He testified that he'd gone down to the jail and interviewed Ake. Although this interview occurred nearly seven years after the event itself, he purported to determine Ake's mental condition at the time of the crime. Dr. von B testified that Ake didn't know the difference between right and wrong. He described Ake as a chronic paranoid schizophrenic. He said Ake heard voices, and that he killed the Rev. and Mrs. Douglass and left their children for dead "to make the voices stop."

The jury didn't buy any of it.

Verdict. The trial went on for a long time. It shouldn't have. This was not a hard case to prove because they had detailed statements from both Ake and Hatch of exactly what they did. They had the Douglass kids. I felt sorry for Brooks and Leslie for being put through the emotional wringer of having to testify again.

The verdict was never in doubt. After four hours of deliberation, the jury found Glen Burton Ake was guilty of murder in the first degree in the deaths of Richard and Marilyn Douglass.

Sentencing. After the first stage in a murder one case that results in a verdict of guilty, we then have a second stage to determine punishment. The jury now goes back and sets the punishment. This is known as the punishment phase. In other words, the jury that has convicted a person of murder is the same jury that determines the sentence.

A bill of particulars has to be filed, called "aggravating circumstances." The Oklahoma legislature establishes what things may be considered aggravating circumstances.

With all the participants assembled back in the courtroom, I told the jury what we were getting ready to do. I said, "I'll give you the proper instructions at the proper time, but you are going to have to determine what penalty you are going to set for Mr. Ake."

A lot of things are admissible in the punishment stage than there are in the first stage. The defense can put on anything that can be considered mitigating. For example, it can bring witnesses who testify to the person's background and character, and why he should be spared the death penalty. They can say he's a good old boy, and stuff like that.

The prosecution, for its part, can bring witnesses to testify how they have suffered as a result of this murder and why this person *should* be put to death. The prosecution can also introduce information on other crimes committed by the defendant--evidence that is excluded from the first stage trial. In the Ake case, for example, District Attorney Stocker could reveal to the jury that Ake and his partner had committed a similar double murder in Texas and were in the process of a robbery when arrested in Colorado.

I turned to the prosecution. "Are you ready to make your opening statement?"

Cathy Stocker said, "The State rests."

I was dumbfounded. She didn't bring anybody in. She had available all those people in the 1980 trial in which Ake was found guilty and received the death penalty. She could have brought in witnesses and the sheriff of Hardin County, Texas, where they did the same thing--killed a couple and stole their car. She could have put on all that stuff out in Colorado, where Ake was caught in the midst of getting ready to murder again.

I said, "What did you say?"

"The State rests."

"That means you're not going to put on any second stage evidence?"

"Yes, your Honor."

I had no choice but to turn to the defense. "Is the defense ready?"

Attorney Irven Box didn't squander his opportunity to argue why Ake should not be executed. He brought back Dr. von Brauchitsch to testify that Ake was insane at the time of the killing. He said Ake didn't know the difference between right and wrong. (Note: That's part of the McNaughton Rule, and that's what Oklahoma follows: "Do you know the difference between right and wrong, and the consequences of your act?")

It was now seven years since the murders took pace. Dr. von B, who had never seen Ake until a few weeks ago, testified that seven years ago Ake didn't know the difference between right and wrong. This was, in my opinion, a bunch of bull. But I had to let him testify to it because of his qualifications as a board-certified psychiatrist.

The jury did the only thing it could do, given the failure of the prosecution to put on evidence of aggravating circumstances. If the prosecuting attorney fails to prove aggravating circumstances, the jury cannot give the death penalty. This jury did the next best thing: it gave Ake two life sentences, plus two 200 year sentences, all to be served consecutively. (Note: At that time, Oklahoma did not have life without the possibility of parole.)

Ake thanked his attorney. "You did one hell of a job," he said.

He left the courtroom wearing leg irons with the jury never aware that he had worn them throughout the trial. He was smiling.

Epilogue. Several weeks later Cathy Stocker called me and asked if she could take me to lunch. We met at the Whitehall Club on the top floor of the Fidelity Bank building. She wanted me to tell why I thought the jury didn't give Ake the death penalty.

I asked, "Do you really want to know? Do you want me to tell you the truth?''

"Yes," she said. "That's why I wanted to have lunch with you."

I said, "It's because you f____d it up!"

"What do you mean?"

"It's because you didn't put on any second stage evidence to show this wasn't a one-time deal, that he did the same thing in Texas and was getting ready to do it again in Colorado. You had all those witnesses available. All you had to do was subpoena them. If you had put them on, you would have got the death penalty if the jury had found out how damned mean he was."

Steven Keith Hatch

Hatch's odyssey through the legal system followed a contorted and circuitous path. His track record from the time he was convicted points to the number of stops a slayer can make on his way to the death chamber.

He was convicted April 1980 in a non-jury trial and received two death sentences. Three years later, the appeals court upheld his conviction but ordered that the punishment phase of Hatch's trial be held again. The court based its ruling on a recent U.S. Supreme Court opinion regarding a Florida case in which a person participated in a crime but did not kill anyone.

Hatch's rehearing on the sentencing phase took place in January 1984. Canadian County District Judge Edward C. Cunningham reimposed the two death sentences. He stated that Steven Hatch's culpability was "absolute under the facts of this case."

Hatch escaped a July 25, 1985, execution with only thirteen hours to spare. Justice Byron White granted a stay until his appeal could be heard by the U.S. Supreme Court. On January 13 the following year, the high court, by a 7 to 2 vote, refused to hear Hatch's appeal.

Meanwhile, Hatch's new attorney--he had gone through several by now--was Thomas M. Lahiff who worked for a New York law firm that specialized in fighting the death penalty. He wanted Judge Chatman removed from the case, so he filed a petition for a type of hearing that is known in legal parlance as "post-conviction relief."

Post-conviction. I presided over the post-conviction hearing on January 26, 1987. Two major determinations came out of the hearing. First, Judge Chatman acknowledged that he should have excused himself from the case because he had assisted in the investigation at the time of the slayings.

Second, I voided Hatch's death sentences and ordered a new penalty trial. I explained, "I cannot ignore what the judge (Chatman) said. The case would have been reversed on appeal in a New York minute."

I ordered Hatch back into court on February 23 for a hearing to determine whether or not he was to die for his part in the robbery-slaying. I emphasized that he remained convicted of the slayings; it was only the penalty phase of the trial that would be reheard.

Penalty phase. By mutual agreement, the trial was held in Oklahoma City rather than Canadian County. Hatch, now 33, was represented by attorney Virgil C. "Chuck" Black, whom I appointed, as well as Thomas Lahiff.

Before the trial, the defense tried to withdraw Hatch's plea for a non-jury trial. He now wanted a jury to set the punishment. But I wouldn't let him. "You've already done it. I see no reason to change that," I said.

The trial was pretty much a repeat of the first trial. The evidence was all the same. Brooks Douglas, now twenty-four, and his sister, Leslie, twenty, both of whom were critically wounded in the robbery-slaying, repeated their testimony of how the family was terrorized by Hatch and Ake for two hours. Leslie testified that both Hatch and Ake tried to rape her as her brother and parents lay tied up on the floor.

Prosecutor Cathy Stocker put a woman named Virginia Anderson on the stand. She testified she traveled with Hatch and Ake when they committed a similar robbery-slaying near Lumberton, Texas. Such testimony of other crimes would not have been admissible in the criminal stage, but it was allowable in a penalty trial.

Defense attorney Chuck Black made a determined effort to show that Hatch was motivated by fear. He portrayed Ake as the main aggressor and triggerman.

The defense paraded a number of Hatch's family members through the witness chair to describe Steven as a "good boy" who had a deprived childhood and was mentally slower than others his age.

Hatch took the stand in his own behalf. "I'm not guilty of murder. I didn't kill anybody," he said. "I'm sorry it happened," he said of the shooting. "I wouldn't have gone if I had known what was going to happen."

Verdict. After hearing all the evidence, I found Hatch guilty and sentenced him to death. It was appealed to the U.S. Supreme Court, and was affirmed.

Epilogue. Steven Keith Hatch was executed at McAlester Prison August 9, 1996, for his role in the Douglass murders seventeen years before. He became the eighth Oklahoma inmate to be executed since the state resumed use of the death penalty in 1990.

This was one of the first cases where the shooter got life and the accomplice was executed.

§ § §

11

Ruling on Rape

To me, rape is a heinous crime. I don't think a woman ever gets over it, not even if she's a sexually experienced woman. It's something that weighs on their minds.

I can't begin to tell you how many rape cases I've tried. I have tried more rape cases than murder cases simply because there are a helluva lot more rapes than murders.

A lot of judges treat rape as a lesser crime, particularly if the woman knew the man beforehand. But I think a woman has an absolute right to say no, even on a date.

Part of the problem is that rape is a hard crime to prove unless it is a violent rape in which the perpetrator injures the girl--hits her, blacks her eye, breaks her jaw, etc. In these cases, the perpetrator leaves visible marks on her body that can be used as corroborating evidence.

Most rapes leave no marks. Very few of them are brutal. One of the things defense lawyers try to do is to show there are no cuts or bruises. Hell, if you put a gun to somebody's head or hold a knife at their throat, those won't leave any scars. Emotional, yes, but not physical.

The only thing a judge can do is instruct the jury that if the perpetrator overcame the woman by force, that constitutes rape.

Psychologists tend to take two different attitudes toward rape. For some, rape is a predominantly sexual act. Others say it stems from a deep hatred towards women.

I think it is a combination of both.

A lot of women think they are somehow at fault. I don't know why. Nevertheless, they seem to think if they had somehow done something different, it wouldn't have happened to them.

I used to offer to talk with rape victims after the trial. I tried to tell them, "It's not your fault."

Erroll Bruner

One would not have thought of Erroll Bruner as a vicious rapist. He was an average-looking guy, average height and weight, wore average clothes, and drove a silver-and-black Cadillac.

Yet he committed one of the most despicable cases of rape I ever tried.

Late in 1972, Bruner was driving down an interstate highway outside Oklahoma City when he spotted two youths, a boy and a girl, both about 18, hitchhiking alongside the interstate on-ramp. He stopped to offer them a ride.

He drove only a few miles before he turned off at an exit where there was an abandoned building that once housed a roadside grocery store. "This is as far as I go," he said.

The couple thanked him. Instead of letting them out, however, Bruner sped up again and drove another mile or so along the access road to an abandoned farmhouse. He told the kids he wanted sex from the girl as payment for the ride.

They, of course, refused. Bruner and the boy got into a fight inside the car. The two got away from Bruner and started running. He caught up with them at a drainage culvert that crossed under the highway. He and the boy began fighting again. The boy broke free and ran. Bruner raped the girl.

He then dragged the girl back to the abandoned farmhouse. Five gang members were waiting there. After raping her again, he threw her down on a dirty mattress on the floor of a back bedroom and let his buddies take turns raping her. They forced her to commit oral and anal sodomy.

Somehow she got loose from them and ran naked to the interstate highway where a passing motorist stopped and saved her from the gang members. This Good Samaritan called the police who came out and picked up Bruner and his pals.

Erroll Bruner's trial came up in my court in June 1973. The others were tried separately. A jury convicted him of first degree rape, and I sentenced him to eighty-five years.

The Reluctant Witness

Sometimes it is not the perpetrator of the crime who incurs the wrath of the court but a witness who refuses to testify. This happened in a 1984 rape trial in which the court had to exercise its power to get a prominent businessman to testify.

One November 1983 evening, Ralph Edward Plotner, a wealthy oilman, joined a well-known doctor, the doctor's girlfriend, and another man for dinner at Joe Kelly's restaurant in Oklahoma City. The doctor and his girlfriend got into a loud and disruptive argument, and the party was asked to leave the restaurant. The doctor was too drunk to drive, so Plotner and the woman drove him home, then Plotner drove the woman to her home in the Nantucket Condominiums in the northwestern part of the city.

She thanked Plotner for the ride home. But apparently he expected more, for he forced himself on her. First, he committed oral sodomy on her against her will and consent. Then, he tried to rape her but was unable to get an erection. He said he would "get her" if she "told" anyone.

As Plotner was positioning himself for other sexual acts, the woman slipped away and ran down the stairs. He caught her at the front door and slammed her to the floor, breaking her arm. Also broken in the struggle was his expensive Rolex watch.

Undoubtedly, Plotner knew the broken watch could be used to identify him, so he thought it might be a pretty good idea to get it fixed. Some people might have gotten rid of such incriminating evidence, but not Ralph Edward Plotner. He was too proud of his $1,200 Rolex to throw it away.

He may have been rich, but that didn't mean he was smart. He gave the telltale watch to an employee of B.C. Clark Jewelers in downtown Oklahoma City to have it repaired. That was a dumb thing to do because, based on the victim's description, a broken Rolex was one of the first things the police went looking for.

Plotner was arrested and bound over for trial.

Barry Albert, assistant district attorney, was the prosecutor. Barry was a big guy, an ex-marine, and a first-rate lawyer. He obtained a *subpoena duces tecum* ("bring with you") for B.C. Clark Jewelers. The subpoena ordered them to appear at the trial and bring with them the watch, the records of what was wrong with it, and a report of what they had to do to repair it.

At his trial, Plotner tried the old, shopworn defense that it was date rape with consent. (That would have gotten him a lesser sentence.) He did not admit to being unable to get an erection. He denied he had his watch cleaned and repaired.

When it came time for rebuttal, Albert asked to approach the bench. The other lawyers joined in a sidebar conference. He said he had a rebuttal witness who had not shown up.

I asked what the witness was expected to testify to. He explained about the Rolex watch and said he planned to introduce it into evidence, inasmuch as the victim had already described her assailant's watch and testified how it got broken in the struggle.

"Why is your witness not here? What excuse did he give?"

"Your Honor, they're claiming some kind of privilege. They say they're not allowed to give out information on customer records. They say they're not coming"

"They said what?" I exclaimed.

"They said they're not coming."

"Did you subpoena them? Was the subpoena served? Have you checked?"

"Yes, it was served by the sheriff," he said.

I turned to my bailiff, "Bring me a phone." She carried a telephone on a long cord to the bench. I sent the jury to the jury room.

I dialed the number for B.C. Clark Jewelers. "Let me talk to B.C. Clark."

The party said, "B.C. Clark is dead."

"Well, let me talk to whoever took his place." A man came on the phone and identified himself as the manager. I asked, "Did Barry Albert have a subpoena served on you to bring a Rolex watch, appear in court, testify, and bring your records?''

He said, ''Yes, he did.''

''Why aren't you up here?''

''Well, I told Mr. Albert that we don't give out information about our customers.''

The store was a block-and-a-half from the courthouse. ''Okay,'' I said. ''You've got two choices. If you'll wait about two minutes, there will be a deputy sheriff there to bring you up here by whatever means is necessary. Bring the watch, the records, and the person who can testify about what has happened to the watch. Your other choice is to walk up here--it's only a block--and bring it yourself. That's the only two choices you've got.''

I added, ''Now, shall I send the sheriff, or are you getting ready to walk out the front door?''

He said, ''I'll be right up, Judge.''

Within ten minutes, we had a witness. Albert put him on the stand. He identified the watch. He identified the defendant as the person who turned it over to him. He testified to the damage to the watch and what they did to fix it.

Plotner was convicted. I sentenced him to a total of 20 years--fifteen for sodomy and five for attempted rape. The five-year sentence was later overturned on a technicality, but the fifteen-year sentence stood.

The broken Rolex, which he was too miserly to throw away, probably was what convicted him. Otherwise, it would have been her words against his, and the jury would have had a hard time convicting him.

On the other hand, his inability to achieve an erection probably worked in his favor. If he had been able to complete the act of rape, he probably would have gotten fifty to sixty years.

David Johns Bryson

Occasionally the scars appear not on the victim but on the perpetrator. Such was the case with David Johns Bryson.

On September 13, 1982, a twenty-year-old legal secretary was entering her car in a downtown Oklahoma City parking lot when she was accosted by a man who was a stranger to her. He was a large person, standing over six feet tall and weighing more than 230 pounds.

He put his hand in his pocket and said, "Move over, Bitch, or I'll blow your face off." Not knowing whether or not he had a gun, she complied.

The man held her head in his crotch and forced her to perform oral sex as he drove to an isolated ravine in the southeastern area of the city.

After stopping the car, he ripped off her blouse and used it to blindfold her. She saw he carried a large hunting knife. He dragged her under a large tree and said, "You'd better not scream or they're going to find your bloody body all over the place."

The man tore off the rest of her clothes, raped her and committed anal sodomy. Then he forced her to perform oral sex again.

The girl was convinced that he was going to kill her, that she was not going to live. So she bit down on his penis as hard as she could.

He began to scream and hit her, but she told him through clenched teeth that she would not let go until he rolled over with his hands beneath him. Then she jumped up and ran, nude, to a nearby housing project where she found help.

David Johns Bryson, 28, was arrested two weeks later. Police investigators were significantly aided by the efforts of a team of volunteers from the YMCA Rape Crisis Center. They got on the phones and called every physician and hospital in the metropolitan area to ask if anyone had sought treatment for a mangled or mutilated penis. Police learned that Bryson had sought treatment for an infected bite.

Spectators packed the courtroom for the four-day trial that began February 7, 1983. Barry Albert was prosecuting attorney.

Bryson was represented by Jim Pearson. He argued that the arrest was illegal because the doctor who tipped the authorities had violated the confidential doctor-patient relationship.

In cross-examining the victim, the defense tried to shake her identification of Bryson. They elicited an admission of how frightened she was during the attack.

Q: "During the time you were under the attacker's control, would that be the most frightening time of your life?" Pearson asked.

A: "Yes," she said.

Obviously, Pearson was hoping the jury would infer that her judgment on that day was impaired by fear.

The state offered into evidence a photograph taken of the defendant's mutilated male organ. The defense attorney jumped up and objected. I asked to see the picture so I could rule.

After viewing the photograph and hearing the testimony, I said, "It is only a photo of a male organ. I'll bet everyone in this courtroom, including the jury, has seen one before. If you have ever seen one, you have seen them all."

The jury of six men and six women deliberated two-and-a-half hours before returning a verdict. They found Bryson guilty of first degree rape, one charge of kidnapping, and three counts of sodomy (two oral and one anal). He was sentenced to a total of eighty-five years in prison--seventy-five for the rape, and four ten-year sentences for the kidnapping and sodomy convictions.

I ordered the seventy-five-year sentence to be served before the four ten-year sentences, which could be served concurrently.

Epilogue #1. After the trial, Bryson sued the doctor who disclosed his injury to the police. He sought $2.5 million in damages, claiming the doctor had betrayed professional ethics and state law by violating doctor-patient confidentiality. The case was tried before District Judge James E. Gullett.

Bryson lost his suit. He appealed to the Oklahoma Supreme Court, where he lost again. The high court ruled that doctor-patient privilege does not protect someone from police investigators, but is restricted only to trial testimony. "Applying this statute in the broad manner urged by appellant would serve as a cloak for crime," the court wrote.

Epilogue #2. In 1999, Bryson's conviction was overturned on the basis of DNA evidence and he won a new trial.

Sadly, the victim, now 36, suffered a stroke within hours of being informed of the DNA results. She died three days later. Bryson remained in jail. He was set for a new trial.

Larry Dale Peninger

In the early morning hours of January 8, 1983, a twenty-one-year-old Edmond, Oklahoma, woman was filling her car with gasoline at a self-service station. A man drove up in a pickup truck and asked directions to a particular restaurant. As she was telling him how to get there, he asked her to come over to his truck so he could write it down.

The man pulled a knife, put it to her throat, and forced her into the truck. They drove off, leaving her car at the pump with the motor running and the nozzle still in the tank. He put a ski mask on her head, backwards, so she couldn't see where they were going.

He took her to a house in far northeastern Oklahoma City and raped her. Then he allowed her to call the gas station to have her car moved and locked. After the call, he forced her to have oral sex.

In what can be described only as a bizarre twist, twice during her ordeal the woman persuaded her attacker to allow her to call her parents. He even spoke to her father himself.

Finally, the woman convinced her attacker that she had a tumor that was erupting and she would die if she didn't get to a hospital right away. Believing her, he started driving toward Mercy Hospital in far northwest Oklahoma City. However, he got lost and took the ski mask off her so she could help him find the hospital.

Then, in a more bizarre twist, he stopped two Edmond police officers to ask directions. The police called an ambulance that took her to the hospital. She asked the ambulance attendant to write down the pickup's license tag number.

Once inside the hospital's examining room, she told a nurse she had been raped.

The next day, police arrested Larry Dale Peninger, 27, at his

Norman, Oklahoma, home after tracing the truck's tag number.

Brought to Oklahoma City, Peninger was identified by his victim and charged with kidnapping, first degree rape, and oral and anal sodomy.

Trial began April 11, 1983. Barry Albert was prosecuting attorney. He told the jury, "In his own sordid way, he [Peninger] not only ravished this woman, he became the ravisher of her family. Because she was blindfolded and didn't know where she was, he was having his own sordid fun, like a cat playing with a mouse."

Peninger testified in his own defense. He told the jury the woman got in his truck voluntarily after the pair struck up a conversation. He said the woman disrobed at a friends house and engaged in a naked "necking session."

Peninger said the woman left the car running with the lights on and the door open next to the pump "as a lark."

The jury didn't buy this cock-and-bull story. They deliberated about two hours before finding him guilty of kidnapping, first degree rape, oral sodomy, and anal sodomy.

The panel set his punishment at 125 years (ten years, seventy-five years, twenty years, and twenty years, respectively).

Epilogue. Two weeks later, Larry Dale Peninger pleaded guilty in my court to abducting and raping another woman the previous December. This became his second conviction in less than a month.

I sentenced him to a total of fifty years for first degree rape, oral sodomy, and kidnapping (thirty, ten and ten, respectively). I ordered the sentences to run consecutively.

Child Molester

The worst kind of rapist, in my mind, is someone who preys on small children. I have two daughters, and I always worried about them.

A preacher appeared in my court in the early 1970s on a charge of molesting his own twelve-year-old daughter and four of her friends. In his statement, he said he had "fallen in love" with his daughter--not as a parent but as a man loves a woman. He took her out to dinner at nice restaurants as if he were courting her. And he had sex with her over an extended period of time.

The police caught him in the act. He had driven down by the Canadian River, pulled off into a secluded lane, parked the car, and began having sex with her. The police in their rounds saw a car down there where it shouldn't be and went to investigate. They walked up to the car, shined their flashlights in the windows, and saw him having intercourse with the girl in the back seat.

He told police the girl actually seduced him, that she was the one who continually suggested sex. (I guess he must have read the book, *Lolita*, in which an aging Lothario is seduced by a young girl.)

When trial was ready to begin, I sent to have the jury brought in. The preacher took one look at those twelve men and women, then had a change of heart. His lawyer announced that his client wished to change his plea from not guilty to guilty. He absolutely did not want to face a jury after raping a bunch of twelve-year-olds.

I sentenced him to five life sentences, one for each child, the sentences to be served consecutively. That meant he would never get out of prison. I wanted him locked up forever.

The disheartened rapist asked, "Why don't you just give me the death penalty?"

"I would if I could," I shot back. (Note: Rape no longer carried the death penalty in Oklahoma.)

The afternoon paper reported he had "thrown himself on the mercy of the court."

When I got home that evening, my teen-age daughters were laughing about the story. One remarked, "He sure made a big mistake when he threw himself on the mercy of Judge Cannon for raping those young girls!"

§ § §

12

Coping with Controversy

A judge has to be able to cope with controversy. His sworn duty is to uphold the law, even if it results in an unpopular decision.

A person who cannot stomach controversy is a person who can be pushed around all over the place. A judge who needs constant approval will end up losing control of the courtroom to whatever high-profile lawyer may be arguing a case before him. For example, William Kunstler tried this gambit in the Nauni murder trial. I didn't fall for it.

Also, I never took a case "under advisement." That's a fancy term some judges use in a non-jury case as a way of saying they're not ready to rule. It may take days or weeks--sometimes even months--before they're ready to make a ruling. I never did that.

"When you quit talking, I'm ready to rule," is what I used to tell the lawyers. After all, I'd heard the whole case. I knew how I was going to rule. So why not give them my ruling right then and there?

School Land Commission

I guess I made more enemies out of the school land case than any other. It also brought me the most satisfaction. The issue had deep roots and high feelings that dated back to when Oklahoma became a state.

Facts. As a condition of statehood, the Enabling Act of 1906 passed by the U.S. Congress granted Oklahoma more than 3.1 million acres of land to benefit public schools. All of the school land was in western Oklahoma in what had been Oklahoma Territory. The state constitution barred the state from using school land trust funds for any purpose other than the school beneficiaries.

Much of the land had been sold off by the 1980s, but about 766,000 acres remained. This land was leased to ranchers and farmers. The revenues from these leases flowed to the School Land Commission for distribution to the proper educational authorities.

The problem was the manner in which the leases were issued and renewed. The leases stayed in the same families as a matter of "privilege," passing from generation to generation, at absurdly low rates. A 1981 audit, for example, indicated rents on school land averaged about one-third the rental obtained on other farmland in the area.

In addition to getting land at absurdly low rates, leaseholders were building houses, barns, and other farm structures on the land as if they owned it. It was a sweetheart deal for those lucky enough to hold a lease, because the Commission would even loan them money at a low interest rate to improve the property.

This was the rankest kind of fraud. The people being defrauded were the schoolchildren of Oklahoma who were supposed to be the beneficiaries. The policy violated the state constitution and the Enabling Act.

Court action. In 1981, the Oklahoma Education Association (OEA) and several participating school districts filed suit in district court in Oklahoma County against the School Land Commission. The suit charged the commission with failure to obtain the maximum rent possible from the land. The OEA alleged that the commission did not solicit bids nor did it obtain realistic appraisals of land before renewing leases. They estimated this practice cost the state school districts about $10 million a year.

The suit was assigned to my court. Before we could hold a hearing, however, the commission filed a lawsuit of its own asking the Oklahoma Supreme Court to step in. It asked for the high court's guidance in the controversy inasmuch as it had been operating under a set of 1966 rules which said it should renew all leases, with or without preference rights, unless a lessee was abusing the land or other unusual circumstances were involved.

The supreme court accepted jurisdiction. It handed down a decision in February 1982 that threw the whole issue into confusion and chaos. The high court voided all existing school land lease laws. The justices said the land was a "sacred trust" to be used for the maximum benefit of state schools. However, the high court did not chart specific methods for assuring that school lands would produce top dollar rents. That little bit of unfinished business now fell back to the lower courts.

Hearings. With the case now back in my court, I set a hearing for March 13. The School Land Commission was comprised of high-ranking state officers, chaired by the governor and including the lieutenant governor, state auditor and inspector, agriculture board president, and superintendent of public instruction.

The commission had already met three times since the supreme court ruling. But the members were obviously unwilling to be pushed into a new program of competitive bidding. The timing was bad, they said. Many loans had been approved but the money had not yet been delivered. Should they fulfill their commitment? And what about taking sealed bids on oil and gas leases?

I wasn't buying the commission's arguments. In terms that left little room for doubt, I warned them that they were proceeding at their own risk if they continued to violate the law. "Kids in this state have been shortchanged for seventy-five years, and now it's time to go the other way."

I told them, "Everybody has forgotten the beneficiaries are the schoolkids of Oklahoma, not the farmers and ranchers."

The commission and I dueled back and forth for the next month as they attempted to come up with an acceptable policy for competitive bidding. I accused them of rigging the new rules in favor of present leaseholders. An auction of 57,000 acres of agricultural leases in Harper and Beaver counties was scheduled for April 19. I issued a temporary injunction halting the process, saying, "There will be no more leases and no more loans of any kind, shape or description...there will be no sale of school land property or school land leases without further order of this court."

They appealed to the Oklahoma Supreme Court, which refused to halt the order. The high court's refusal to act, in effect, let stand my temporary restraining order.

The conflict rose to a new pitch on April 26 when I ruled the commission's recent attempt to revamp its rules was illegal. I gave the commission until June 16 to come up with a plan to draw the largest number of eligible bidders while generating the best cash return for school districts. "The party is over," I said. The commission's latest efforts to revise its leasing system still favored ranchers and farmers and amounted to nothing more than "just a new way to skin the same cat."

Politics of privilege. In a blatant attempt to bring pressure on the court, an angry group of more than 200 ranchers and farmers jammed the state House of Representatives on June 4 to air their gripes. They criticized competitive bidding proposals and urged continued preference rights for current leaseholders. Others maintained that soil conservation would go out the window if the land is put to auction. One man went so far as to claim that if schoolchildren are being cheated by the system, "it is not the leaseholders that are doing it, but the quality of public education in the state."

Perhaps the most outlandish assertion was the one brought by a leaseholder who claimed that leaseholders are, in effect, "state employees." He insisted that "no part of the state government lets jobs to the lowest bidders as is proposed for farmers and ranchers.''

Dueling judges. A flanking attack was made by five leaseholders in western Oklahoma. They pitted judge against judge.

Suit was filed in Texas, Beaver, Cimarron, and Harper counties that would nullify my ruling. The case was assigned to Judge Frank Ogden whose district included those counties. (Note: Ogden had been our floor leader in the House of Representatives during Edmondson's administration.) This marked the first time I know of where one district judge has tried to overrule another district judge.

When I heard what they did, I issued an injunction against Ogden. I said this was "forum shopping" of the worst order.

They took it to the Oklahoma Supreme Court. The high court sustained me. They told Ogden to get out because he had no jurisdiction. Jurisdiction, they said, was in Oklahoma County in front of Judge Cannon.

I didn't blame Frank Ogden. If I had been out there in western Oklahoma, I probably would have done the same thing. I have always felt a judge should be answerable to the people he judges.

Sticking point. The School Land Commission asked for a postponement of my June 16 deadline for coming up with a new plan. One of the points they hadn't been able to resolve was the question, who owned the improvements made on the property--the leaseholder or the state? We reset the hearing to July 7.

The ownership of improvements issue can perhaps be summarized in a conversation I had with one of the owners of Jude and Jody Furniture store. They were good friends of mine. We'd been on boat trips together. Jody called me and took me to lunch during the time this debate was raging. It seems he was the holder of a large school land lease and he wanted me to not take it away from him.

I told him, "Jody, I'm sorry, but I'm going to."

He was incredulous. "That's where I live. I've built a home on it...barns...and fences...."

"Then it all belongs to the state now," I avowed.

I nearly lost a friend over that, but I didn't. We maintained our friendship.

But those guys out west, the representatives and senators, they really got on my butt. I made some real enemies out of that. Too bad.

Bring in the feds. The next attempt to block me came in the form of a suit filed in federal court. Seventeen leaseholders, acting on behalf of all renters, filed a class-action lawsuit.

The suit sought to void the actions I had taken. Named in the suit, besides me, were all nine members of the Oklahoma Supreme Court, the state's attorney general, and the five members of the School Land Commission.

The case was assigned to U.S. District Judge Ralph G. Thompson. He declined to intervene and eventually dismissed the suit.

Confrontation. By the close of business on July 7, 1982, the School Land Commission presented me with a new plan. The twenty-seven-page document was a sore disappointment. I characterized it as containing the same old sentiments in fresher type.

I rejected the plan in a July 9 hearing, saying the rules still favored leaseholders at the detriment of school children. I ordered the commission to draft a completely new set of rules by the following Monday, or I would rewrite the regulations myself. Monday was three days hence. It happened to be the last day the legislature would meet that year, and state law required the rules to be adopted while the legislature was in session.

"I don't intend to let this land go to pot and the schoolchildren's money go down the drain just because you won't act," I said. "But if the commission doesn't do its constitutional duty, I'm going to do it for you."

By holding their toes to the fire, so to speak, I was not only risking the wrath of senators and representatives of the western counties, I was also taking on the governor, lieutenant governor, and three cabinet-level officials who comprised the School Land Commission.

Sparring continued for the next several weeks between the courtroom and the commission's meeting room as I tried to get the commission to adhere to leasing guidelines I deemed constitutional. The sticking point continued to be the fate of permanent improvements made to leased property.

My patience ran out. I ruled on September 23 at the end of a long day's hearing that all improvements built on state land leases since statehood will become the property of the state when leases expire. The ruling was to become effective immediately and covered everything from fences to barns to leaseholders' homes.

"You can't build on someone else's land. It's just not that simple," I declared.

Resolution. Lease auctions began in March 1983. The first round of competitive bidding astounded everyone. Prices came in three times higher than the old prices, and 203 percent higher than minimum bid prices set by appraisers.

Despite the collusion of some farmers who refrained from bidding out of deference to their friends and neighbors, the state's revenues were increased by nearly $3 million by year's end.

The final chapter was written December 1985 when the Oklahoma Supreme Court issued an opinion on the controversial lawsuit. The high court affirmed my ruling that permanent improvements on leased school land belonged to the state School Land Commission, and leaseholders did not have an automatic right to renew leases.

Epilogue. Lawyers for the School Land Commission tell me that from the time of my ruling until the present time, the income has increased by $4 million a year. That totals to more than $60 million in additional revenues since 1983 that they have received for the common schools.

Moreover, the School Land Commission now administers a trust fund of $1.2 billion.

National Guard to Honduras

Throughout the mid 1980s, American public opinion was sharply polarized over the civil war in Nicaragua. The U.S.-backed Contras were seeking to overthrow the Communist-backed Sandinista government. Rebel Contra groups operated out of bases located in neighboring Honduras.

Peace activists vigorously protested President Ronald Reagan's support of the Contras. They decried what they called the "Vietnamization" of the conflict there.

Protesters. Thus when it was announced in September 1986 that units of the Oklahoma National Guard would go to Honduras for four weeks of training in November, protesters stormed the state Capitol. They demanded that Governor Nigh rescind his approval of sending two National Guard units to Honduras.

Naturally, it made headlines in the media when leaders of several groups held a press conference at the Capitol. They viewed the sending of guard units as an attempt by Reaganites to circumvent congressional limits on troop deployment in the area. "To send guard units to Honduras now would lend tacit support to a policy which kills Nicaragua civilians and gives America a black eye in the court of world opinion," they said.

Complaint. A group of twenty-two people who identified themselves as "Oklahomans for Justice in Central America" filed a lawsuit to prohibit Governor George Nigh from sending National Guard units to Honduras. They described themselves as state taxpayers. Attorney Doug Parr represented them. (Parr previously was defense attorney in the Rita Silk Nauni case.)

The suit charged that the National Guard "will deliver or abandon [artillery] equipment to the use of military forces seeking to overthrow the government of the sovereign state of Nicaragua."

Further, the suit said, "The dispatch of units of the Oklahoma National Guard to Honduras...is a violation of Oklahoma law in that the true purpose of the assignments is not for training exercise as authorized by law and, in addition, the action complained of is not authorized by state or federal law."

Disposition. The case was assigned to my court. Because of the urgency of the situation--the first troops were scheduled to depart October 26--I set a hearing for October 23.

Governor Nigh was represented by the Oklahoma Attorney General's office. On his behalf, the attorney general filed a motion to dismiss the lawsuit. The governor's motion challenged the legal standing of the twenty-two plaintiffs, saying this was not a state tax issue because all funds involved were from the federal government. The motion also contended the National Guard units were not called into service by Governor Nigh but by the U.S. Secretary of the Army with Nigh's consent.

I threw out the case, holding that the taxpayer group lacked legal standing to file such a suit "just because they are state taxpayers." I also said state courts cannot interfere with military decision.

"In my opinion, Governor Nigh has the authority to train the Oklahoma National Guard in or out of the state," I declared. "Whether it is paid for by the state or by the federal government is, in my opinion, immaterial."

I didn't find anything illegal about Governor Nigh or President Reagan training the Oklahoma National Guard in Honduras.

Ethics Commission

Beginning in 1986, lobbyists and political candidates had to comply with a new ethics commission created by the Oklahoma legislature. One of the first persons to run afoul of the new regulations was gubernatorial candidate David Walters.

Walters, of Oklahoma City, secured loans totaling $162,500, using his house as collateral, to make a final advertising push in his primary bid for the Democratic nomination for governor. The problem was that he obtained the funds from private individuals rather than a commercial financial institution, which the law required. He borrowed $125,000 from a building contractor and $12,500 each from three other individuals.

Attorney General Mike Turpen, the losing candidate, lodged a formal complaint with the newly created state Ethics Commission asking the commission to rule on the legality of the non-bank loans.

Turpen said, "The law is very clear...that no person can give a loan over $5,000 to any candidate for public office." Further, the law defines a campaign contribution as money "or any other thing of value whatsoever which is given or loaned to be used in a campaign for or against...any candidate."

Based on this definition, Turpen charged that the first $5,000 of the $125,000 loan (which came from a building contractor) was a legal contribution, the rest was an illegal contribution. He noted that the mortgages were not filed with the county clerk until September 10 when the loans became public knowledge.

Referral. Under the state's new ethics act, the commission had the authority to (a) dismiss the complaint, or (b) refer it to the Oklahoma County district attorney for possible filing of charges.

On October 6, one month before the general election, the Ethics Commission voted 7 to 0 to refer the complaint against Walters to District Attorney Bob Macy for action. The panel's action came at the end of a six-hour, closed-door investigation.

David Walters then filed a lawsuit challenging the commission's decision to refer the complaint to the district attorney. Macy immediately disqualified himself because he and Walters shared the same campaign manager. Attorney Thomas I Enis was retained as special counsel for the commission.

Argument. Because of the urgency to resolve this complaint, which could affect the outcome of the governor's race, I convened a three-judge panel. We met in a rare evening session on October 13. My colleagues on the bench were Raymond Naifeh and Charles Owens.

David Walters was represented by Robert J. "Jim" Turner and Charles Green. Thomas Enis represented the commission. The attorneys agreed that the facts of the case were not in dispute.

Jim Turner argued that the state's new ethics code was unconstitutional in two areas. First, the commission violated Walters' due process rights when it referred the complaint to the district attorney "for action."

Second, Charles Green argued that the commission "unduly restricts the right of a candidate to spend his own money, and this is unconstitutional."

We recessed after two-and-a-half hours of testimony. I announced we would deliver our opinion at 3:00 p.m. the following day.

Ruling. A standing-room-only crowd of campaign sympathizers, media hounds, and other hangers-on packed the courtroom to await our ruling.

"The loans were legal," I announced to the assembled crowd.

We said the commission violated Walters' procedural due process rights in its investigation October 6 that led to its referral to the district attorney.

Perhaps more significant, we declared as unconstitutional that portion of the ethics act that prohibited a candidate from using the proceeds of non-bank loans in his campaign.

The ruling stated, in part, "The interpretation placed on the loans by the Oklahoma Ethics Commission is an unconstitutional interpretation in violation of the First Amendment of the United States Constitution.

"A person may, under the law, give his own money or property to his campaign and there is no limit on that amount...and that's what the facts of this case were."

We concluded, "The action of the Oklahoma Ethics Commission against David Walters is set aside as null and void. The commission is restrained and enjoined from any other proceedings in connection with these loans against David Walters in this case."

The ruling sparked an immediate uproar. Supporters called the ruling "good news." Opponents were quick to point out the dire consequences. "The floodgates are now wide open for corruption in Oklahoma again," one said. Detractors also noted that I, like Walters, was a Democrat and running for reelection.

Epilogue. The controversy did not end with our ruling. The Ethics Commission filed an immediate appeal with the state supreme court.

The high court waited to take up the case until after the general election in November had concluded. David Walters lost to Henry Bellmon. On the other hand, I won my bid for reelection.

The supreme court took oral arguments on June 9, 1987. It handed down its ruling October 28, nearly a year after the election.

The justices struck down my ruling on David Walters and reopened the possibility for criminal charges being filed against him.

On the one hand, the court's opinion stated I exceeded my authority in ruling three weeks before the 1986 general election that the four non-bank loans totaling $162,500 to Walters were legal. On the other hand, the court itself did not address the legality of those loans.

The net effect of the supreme court decision was to breath new life into the state Ethics Commission. Accordingly, the commission reinstated its complaint against Walters.

Governor Henry Bellmon appointed a special prosecutor in April 1988, Tulsa attorney Lou Bullock. Both District Attorney Bob Macy and Attorney General Robert Henry were disqualified, so that left Bullock in charge of deciding whether or not to file criminal charges against Walter.

Special prosecutor Bullock presented a fourteen-page report to Governor Bellmon on September 19 that year. He concluded that although David Walters clearly violated the law by accepting $162,500 in loans from a few wealthy contributors, no charges should be filed because the law was unconstitutional at that time.

"Without question, David Walters violated the terms of the Oklahoma Ethics Commission Act," he wrote. But "a prosecution against David Walters cannot reasonably be expected to result in a conviction."

Accordingly, "it is determined that this matter is closed, and no further action taken."

In the final analysis, and despite the supreme court's ruling, I felt vindicated by the special prosecutor's ruling.

Clifford Henry Bowen

People get upset at a judge when he sets a convicted murderer free. I put myself in the eye of the storm when, in July 1987, I made a ruling that resulted in triple-murderer Clifford Henry Bowen walking free.

Bowen had been convicted of the contract killing of three men at the Guest Inn motel in Oklahoma City July 7, 1980. It was thought to be drug-related. The motel's night manager, Mary Lee Chilton, identified Bowen as the hitman in the gangland-style triple slaying around the motel pool. Bowen was given three death penalties.

I did not conduct the original trial. Judge Raymond Naifeh did. The 10th Circuit reversed the conviction and ordered a new trial on grounds that District Attorney Bob Macy's office had withheld crucial evidence relevant to the defense. Judge Naifeh died November 29, 1986, and the case landed in my lap.

Bowen was defended by Steven Taylor of McAlester and Jack Zimmerman, partner of famed Texas lawyer Richard "Racehorse" Haynes. Bob Ravitz later told me that when Taylor and Zimmerman found out I was assigned to the case, they were thinking about moving the case to a new venue because of the intense publicity in Oklahoma City. They asked him what kind of judge I was. They had heard I was a law-and-order judge.

Ravitz said he told them they were "walking in luck" because I was the only judge in the courthouse who had the guts to turn an accused triple-murderer free. But they had better be right about the law.

The only eyewitness was now dead. Macy wanted to use the transcript of her testimony from the first trial. The defense objected, saying that the woman had undergone hypnosis while being interrogated by the police. They filed a motion to dismiss. I set a hearing on the motion.

I asked Mr. Macy if he could prove his case without the testimony of the hypnotized woman. He said no, they could not. I told him that if I let the woman's testimony in and Bowen was convicted again, the 10th Circuit would reverse it again. Besides,

I agreed that a hypnotized witness was not a reliable witness to make a positive identification of a person.

I dismissed the evidence. Bob Macy then dropped the prosecution of Bowen.

Macy, who had often cited the conviction of Bowen as his greatest accomplishment as district attorney, was quoted as saying, "I'm sick at my stomach."

Footnote. Clifford Henry Bowen, then 56, moved back to Texas. Several years later, one of his lawyers told me he died. He said Bowen was not the man who killed those three people. Since Bowen was now dead, his lawyer would have no reason to lie.

§ § §

13

Tangling with Torts

A tort is a wrongful act that results in injury or damage to someone's person or property. The objective of tort law is to compensate the injured person for his or her loss.

Running a red light is not a tort. It is a crime for which you might have to pay a fine, but you can't get sued for it. The same can be said for reckless driving.

However, if you run a red light or drive recklessly and you hurt someone, that is a tort and you can be sued. The tort has to be the proximate cause of the injury.

There are torts set out by statute, and there are torts set out by common law. Oklahoma has both. (Note: Statutes are laws enacted by the legislature; common law is that made by the courts.)

Strict Liability

A thirty-two-year-old man died March 3, 1971, in Pauls Valley, Oklahoma. Two years earlier he had been exposed to radioactive iodine, and his widow sued his employer, Halliburton Services, for $1 million for wrongful death. She contended he died as a result of contamination from the nuclear materials he used in his work.

The 1974 trial was held in my court. It was the first case in Oklahoma that involved damages from atomic energy. Oklahoma law--both statutory and common--was silent on this subject and lacked an effective way to deal with damage from atomic energy.

Our courts were "behind the curve," so to speak, when it came to technological advancements.

Halliburton brought in a flock of engineers to prove the company was not negligent. They testified this was the way they always performed this operation, they followed established guidelines in handling this material, nobody did anything wrong, a pipe didn't break, nothing happened to make it happen, and this was just one of those things that happened.

Midway through the seven-day trial, Halliburton lawyers asked me to rule that the plaintiff had to show Halliburton was negligent.

I wrote a long opinion on the matter and filed it with the case so it could be circulated to other judges. I ruled that this was a case of "strict liability." In other words, the aggrieved party does not have to prove negligence. The fact that they're working with a dangerous substance makes the employer liable. All the jury has to do is determine the amount of damages.

I likened it to having a tiger in your back yard. If the tiger gets out of his cage and hurts someone, you are strictly liable for whatever damages he caused. The mere fact of having a dangerous animal in your back yard--no matter how secure the cage--makes you responsible.

I proposed that atomic energy be handled as a separate area of law. More importantly, I suggested that the legal doctrine of "strict liability" be applied to hazardous materials.

In essence, I proposed that whenever an ultra-hazardous material such as radiation is used, the firm or individual in control of the material should be held liable for damages without respect to negligence or precautionary measures taken.

"So if you were using radiation or dynamite, for example, you're responsible for any consequences--negligence doesn't have to be proven," I wrote.

On the other hand, I said, "you have to prove that the material caused the injury before you can collect--you can't assume it."

The jury found for the defendant. I didn't think they should, but they did.

Kerr-McGee

The concept of strict liability for ultra-hazardous materials surfaced again in a 1986 case involving Sequoyah Fuels Corp., a subsidiary of Kerr-McGee Corporation. This was the first atomic energy explosion case in Oklahoma.

Facts. On January 4, 1986, a cylinder ruptured at the Sequoyah Fuels Corp., spilling a toxic cloud over a large area. Eighty-five landowners in the affected area brought suit for $100 million. Named in the suit were Sequoyah Fuels, Kerr-McGee Corp., and Trinity Industries, maker of the cylinder.

Kerr-McGee was engaged in the business of mining uranium in New Mexico. The uranium ore was called ''yellow cake.'' It was shipped in 55-gallon barrels to its subsidiary plant, Sequoyah Fuels, near Gore, Oklahoma, for processing.

The yellow cake, by itself, was not dangerous. It was not yet what we normally thought of as being nuclear energy material.

The Sequoyah Fuels plant processed the ore into a liquid called uranium hexaflouride, otherwise known as UF6. This was an intermediary product in the production of nuclear reactor fuel. At this stage, it was a dangerous and highly volatile fluid.

After processing, the UF6 was loaded into tank cars and shipped to Oak Ridge, Tennessee, or some other plant to be manufactured into fuel rods that powered nuclear energy plants. These rods might end up at such places as Oklahoma Gas and Electric or a nuclear-powered submarine or aircraft carrier. The cylinders to hold the UF6 were made by Trinity Industries of Texas according to specifications drawn by Kerr-McGee.

One of the 5,000-gallon cylinders blew up with a tremendous force. A toxic cloud spewed several thousand feet into the air and drifted in a southeasterly direction. It caused damage to land, homes and people for nearly forty miles.

Ruling. On March 4, 1988, I made a ruling in the case that was considered to be a landmark ruling. I ruled that Sequoyah Fuels was "strictly liable" for any damages because work at the company's uranium-processing plant was "ultra-hazardous." That left it up to the jury to determine how much damages, if any, each landowner had from the toxic cloud.

I wrote, "The use of radioactive materials should be encouraged for the benefit of Oklahoma and the nation, but those who do use and develop it should not only know of the benefits of this miracle energy but the responsibilities to others that goes along with it."

In effect, I was saying if you're in a dangerous business and you hurt someone, you've got to pay. The injured party still has to prove he's been harmed, but he doesn't have to prove you're negligent.

Kerr-McGee was represented by attorney Burck Bailey who said my ruling would be followed in other lawsuits, particularly if the Oklahoma Supreme Court upheld it. Similarly, the landowners' lawyers, John W. Norman and Emmanuel Edem, said they would ask the supreme court to review the ruling "in order not to do this twice." If they waited until after the trial and the supreme court decided my position was wrong, they didn't want to go through a second trial.

In other action, I dismissed the landowners' claim against Trinity Industries. Their attorney, Earl Mills, produced documentation to show the tank had been built to the specifications provided by Kerr-McGee.

I also ruled that landowners not exposed to radiation cannot seek damages for "cancerphobia," fear of getting cancer.

It was amazing to me how many would-be plaintiffs crawled out of the woodwork. Thousands of people claimed they were driving down Interstate 40 that day and were contaminated by the blast. Investigation revealed that most of these people were not even in Oklahoma, let alone on I-40 near the plant. I threw these people out of the case.

Settlement. Following my rulings, the parties agreed to a settlement out of court. The case was dismissed without going to trial. It was a sealed settlement, and the parties were forbidden to discuss the amounts.

This case served as a precedent of law for nuclear energy in Oklahoma.

At times, I wish the case had been tried because it would have made an extremely interesting trial. It was handled by three outstanding lawyers who were well prepared and did a good job for their clients. Being a trial judge can be a great pleasure when you have good attorneys.

Also, there is another reason why I wish the case had been tried. It would have qualified as a "case of first impression." Because the case was settled, however, my ruling never made it up the appellate system. Consequently, it did not become binding on anyone, even though it was new.

Tom Lee v. Volkswagen

The 1977 trial of Tom Lee v. Volkswagen was what is known in legal parlance as a "case of first impression." That means the issue has never been decided by the courts in this state before.

In order to be classified as a first impression case, it has to be appealed and upheld by the appellate court. One district judge cannot bind another district judge's ruling. But if it goes to the supreme court and they rule, then it becomes the law of the state.

The "first impression" aspect of Tom Lee v. Volkswagen was a doctrine known as "second collision." This was the first "second collision" case in Oklahoma. It gets its name from the fact that the person is injured in a second collision or impact that results from the first collision.

Summary. Tom Lee, 16, was on his way to school on April 24, 1974, when his 1964 Volkswagen was struck by another car. The initial impact was relatively minor. However, Lee was thrown out of the vehicle and his head struck the ground with such force that it broke his neck, severed his spinal cord, and left him paralyzed from the neck down.

When Tom Lee's VW was run into by another vehicle, that was the first collision. When the doors flew open and Lee hit the pavement and broke his neck, that was the second collision. There were two separate actions, two separate injuries. I researched the matter and learned it had been determined in other states, but never in Oklahoma.

On September 5, 1975, Tom Lee filed suit against Volkswagen and the woman whose car struck his. After numerous delays and extensive depositions, trial commenced October 19, 1977.

His attorney, John Norman, was a damned good tort lawyer. Norman showed films of simulated crashes wherein another car hit a VW and its doors flew open. He also showed films of a day in the life of Tom Lee, what he could and couldn't do and how he maneuvered around in his automated wheelchair.

Lee's complaint against Volkswagen was based on the company's failure to install an interlocking safety latch on the vehicle which could have prevented the door from opening, a known hazard.

The 1964 model Volkswagen was purchased new by Tom Lee's father in November 1963. It was manufactured in Germany for sale in the United States.

For the previous ten years, more or less, American and some European automobile manufacturers had been making their vehicles with interlocking safety latches. The purpose of the safety latch was to prevent doors from coming open in an accident.

In 1960, fully three years before the manufacture of the Lee car, Volkswagen recognized this need and had begun to incorporate the safety device on other model VWs sold in Europe. But for some inexplicable reason, it wasn't until April 1965 that Volkswagen began to install the safety latch on its Type I "Beetle" sold in the United States. The Lee automobile was a Type I "Beetle" and consequently did not have an interlocking safety latch.

Volkswagen sent over engineers from Germany to testify. They, of course, denied there was anything wrong with the vehicle's design.

Attorney John Norman summed up his argument as follows:

1. The Lee Volkswagen, without an interlocking safety latch, was ten years behind its time in terms of safety.

2. The Lee Volkswagen could have had interlocking capability if Volkswagen had added a 35-cent piece of metal.

3. While involved in a relatively minor intersection accident, both doors of the Lee Volkswagen came open.

4. Tom Lee was ejected from the right door of the Volkswagen, somersaulted on the pavement, and his neck was broken.

5. The Lee Volkswagen, without an interlocking safety latch, was defective.

6. The Lee Volkswagen, without an interlocking safety latch, was unreasonably dangerous.

7. The unreasonably dangerous defect caused Tom Lee's quadraplegia.

8. An interlocking safety latch like Volkswagen installed on other VWs in 1961, three years before they made the Lee VW, would have kept the doors closed.

Resolution. After a month of trial, the jury returned a verdict on November 10, 1977. It found for Tom Lee and awarded him $1.8 million.

I added $235,000 for pre-judgment interest, and entered final judgment in the amount of $2,035,000 against the defendants.

The case was appealed, my ruling was upheld, and "second collision" tort became the law of the state.

Comparative Negligence

Oklahoma was one of the last states to adopt the principle of "comparative negligence." It used to be that the party who hit you had to be 100% negligent. If you were even 1% contributorily negligent, you couldn't collect a dime in Oklahoma. It had been that way since statehood.

I was one of the ones who helped persuade the legislature to change the law to recognize comparative negligence. I went around and buttonholed a bunch of plaintiff's lawyers who were in the legislature. I got their interest, they got a committee together, and they held hearings. I testified in one of the hearings about how bad it was. I showed them how many states had changed to comparative negligence.

I told them it wasn't fair to have one guy 1% at fault, the other party 99% at fault, and the 1% guy doesn't get anything.

I gave them an example about a case I had as a plaintiff's lawyer before I became a judge. My client was an older black lady whose car was hit by another car. She didn't do a damned thing wrong. But she was badly injured and her car was totaled.

It was brought out in court that she didn't have a driver's license. Now, her lack of a license didn't have anything to do with the wreck. It wasn't the proximate cause. She didn't cross the centerline. She didn't do anything wrong.

But the jury found that there was some degree of negligence on her part, and she didn't get anything.

I told them what the defense lawyer told the jury in summing up. "If you find she did anything wrong, one single iota of evidence that she did anything wrong, the law says she's not entitled to recovery."

It was a bad law. Fortunately, the legislature changed it.

After the law was changed, Charlie Owens and I used to go around the state lecturing judges and lawyers on the new law of comparative negligence. We spoke at judges' conferences, legal meetings, and wherever we could find an audience.

We wrote instructions to the jury, we made color-coded verdict forms. We told them, for example, "If you find that both the plaintiff and the defendant were negligent, use the blue form. Everybody that helped cause the wreck, you write in their percentage of negligence, and the numbers have to add up to 100 percent."

Charlie always opened the meeting by saying something like, "We're going to study the new Comparative Negligence Act, and we've been doing this around the state for lawyers and judges."

He would introduce us as, "This is the salt and pepper team. Cannon is Pepper and I'm Salt." (Charlie, of course, was black.) That always drew big laugh.

§ § §

14

Bordering on the Bizarre

Some cases would be funny if they didn't carry such overtones of tragedy. I've seen it happen a lot in court, including murder cases, where a witness says something on the stand that causes everybody to laugh--the audience, the jury, the judge, and the staff. The witness may not have intended it to be funny, it just came out that way.

Just because something sounds funny doesn't mean it's not serious. For example, I had a black youth on trial for raping his mother. He insisted on being his own lawyer. I tried to talk him out of it, including reminding him of that old saying, "He who tries to be his own lawyer has a fool for a client." But he wouldn't listen.

The victim took the stand. When it came time to cross-examine her he asked, "How did you know it was me? It was dark in there."

Immediately the audience burst into laughter over the stupidity of such a question. He had clearly implicated himself. When the laughter died down, his mother answered, "Why, I know'd you all your life. You're my son!"

That was tragic as hell, yet it was funny.

Spattered Silicone

Dr. William A. Crockett of Oklahoma City was married to a shapely lady. Carol Sue Crockett's curvaceous figure had been enhanced by the art of the plastic surgeon's knife. In a word, she had silicone breast implants.

Apparently, Dr. Crockett thought he wasn't the only person enjoying those breasts, for the couple separated and were seeking a divorce. She moved into an apartment with friends.

On the evening of March 24, 1974, he went to the apartment where his wife was staying and forced her at gunpoint to leave with him. He drove out to Lake Hefner where he parked the car and tried to persuade her to reconcile with him. They got into a heated argument. He had a gun and, whether by intent or accident, he shot her.

The bullet passed through both breasts, striking the implant, and silicone and blood spattered all over the car. They thought she was fatally wounded although, as later determined, the bullet passed in front of her rib cage.

Dr. Crockett drove his wife to the emergency room at Baptist Hospital. At the same time, police went searching for him when they received word of the shooting.

Officer Jack Wells found Crockett in the treatment room, bending over his wife on a table as other hospital workers treated her. When Crockett saw the policeman, he straightened up and raised his pistol. Officer Wells assumed Crockett was going to shoot somebody, so he shot Crockett in the chest with his own service revolver.

I guess if one has to be shot, he could not pick a better place than an emergency room where doctors and life-saving equipment are immediately available. In Crockett's case, the other doctors promptly went to work saving his life.

Trial. In due course, the matter came to trial. Crockett was charged with assault with a deadly weapon with intent to kill. Mrs. Crockett refused to aid in the prosecution of her husband. She said they had reconciled their differences.

Dr. Crockett took the stand in his own defense. He testified he was desperate and had no intention of shooting Officer Wells. Rather, he intended to shoot himself. He believed his wife's wounds were fatal and he said he felt he had nothing left to live for.

He said when he saw Wells enter the emergency room, he knew he would have to shoot himself quickly before the police took the gun away from him. He asserted he was raising the gun to point it at his own head when Wells shot him.

Mistrial. Crockett's trial ended when I declared a mistrial because of jury error.

After deliberating twelve hours, the jury returned with an oral report that they reached a verdict--not guilty--on the crime with which Crockett was charged. The foreman stated that the panel was deadlocked 7 to 5 on whether Crockett was guilty of a lesser, or included, offense--that of assault with a dangerous weapon.

I declared a mistrial. I ruled that only if a jury is unable to reach a verdict on the higher offense, can it consider the lesser crime. In this case, the jury had reached a verdict on the higher offense and should not have considered the lesser crime.

Dr. Crockett lucked out. I subsequently ruled that to try him again would be double jeopardy under the U.S. Constitution.

Oversized Implants

Some cases should never go to trial. This was one of them.

A woman filed suit against a plastic surgeon for making her breasts too large. She claimed she was embarrassed to go out in public and was asking several hundred thousand dollars in damages.

When she came into my courtroom, what I saw was a very nice-looking woman about five-foot-two in height, weighing 105 pounds, and with breasts like watermelons. Hell, as small as she was, they could have put a couple of lemons in there and she would still have been top-heavy.

We went through the process of picking a jury. When I saw that we had come up with a jury panel of twelve men, I called the lawyers to the front for a bench conference.

"Are you sure you want to try this case?" I asked. "It's going to take two to three days for a malpractice case. You're going to have to put on all your expert witnesses to show what damages she thinks she has had done to her, and all that."

Then I said, "Look at that jury. You've got twelve men sitting on that panel. And you're going to argue to these twelve men that the doctor has made her breasts too big?

"It's going to cost a lot of money to try this case, and I'll bet the jury won't be out fifteen minutes. Is there any chance you can take some kind of settlement?"

The lawyers insisted, "Oh no, Judge, we want to try it."

I said, "Okay, we'll try it. But you're just wasting everybody's time, effort, and money."

Well, we tried it. I was right. The jury wasn't out more than fifteen minutes--I don't know how they had time to vote for a foreman, let alone debate the issue.

They found for the defendant. The woman and her lawyers took nothing. After the jury left, I told her lawyers, "I tried to tell you guys, but you wouldn't listen."

It was a total waste of time. I hated to spend valuable court time on something I knew wasn't going anywhere. But you just can't convince trial lawyers. They love the sound of their own voices.

Displaced Nipples

Late one night in 1988, a young nurse was driving home from her hospital shift when an oncoming car crossed the median and struck her car head-on. The impact threw her straight forward into the steering wheel. Her car was not equipped with an airbag.

The woman's left breast struck the steering wheel with such force that her implant was displaced in such a way that her nipple pointed outward to the side rather than straight ahead. She sued for damages.

Don Manners was her attorney. He sought to introduce a number of photographs taken before and after the injury.

Normal court procedure require a witness to identify a photograph before it can come into evidence. The lawyer can't do this himself; he needs someone to identify it, either the person of whom the picture is taken or the person who took the picture.

Manners was introducing a whole string of photographs taken by the plastic surgeon that showed her breasts before surgery and after surgery. He showed her each picture and she identified it as being her. Pretty soon we had a whole row of tits, tits, and more tits. When he came to one photograph, however, she piped up and said, "That's not a picture of my breast!"

Manners was taken aback. "It was taken by the plastic surgeon. It's got to be your breast."

"No, it's not," she said.

He still persisted, but she was adamant.

"Manners," I said, "she ought to know better than anyone else whether it is a picture of her breast or not. Get on with it."

I then added, "I have spent four years in the Marine Corps with two-and-a-half years in the South Pacific where women wore no tops. I have been to Bourbon Street in New Orleans where women bare their breasts at Mardi Gras. In all those years, I have never seen a breast that looked like that.

"But if she says this is not a picture of her breast, that's good enough for me. The picture will not be taken into evidence."

The jury found for the nurse and awarded her $25,000.

Ben Wiley Jones, Jr.

Sometimes a crook is too smart for his own good. They think they've thought up the perfect crime, but they get tripped up by their own mistakes. Ben Wiley Jones, Jr., was no exception.

In July 1973, Jones was a nineteen-year-old black youth in the Oklahoma County jail on a robbery charge. He didn't like it there, but he was street-smart and struck upon a way to get out of jail. He would become a snitch.

He contacted the district attorney's office, saying he had information on a counterfeiting ring that was operating in the area. The DA's office, in turn, passed on Wiley's offer to the U.S.

Secret Service.

Agents worked out a deal with Jones. If Jones would supply them with information on the counterfeiting ring, the district attorney would arrange to get him back out on the street.

That's the way things work in law enforcement. The detective develops a snitch out of someone who is in trouble with the law, and in exchange for information the detective helps the snitch. Snitches are usually outlaws who run with other outlaws, so they are usually "in the know" about who did what and when.

Ben Wiley Jones, Jr., failed to live up to his end of the bargain. He stole a bicycle and skipped town before being hauled back into court on the burglary charge. Before leaving, however, he called his mother and girlfriend and told them, "If I die, don't worry. I'll be back."

Jones had a scheme to fake his own death. He singled out another black youth of similar size and weight. On August 12, 1973, he lured Reuben Ellis, 14, to the Sooner Inn motel in south Oklahoma City, where he killed him. Ellis didn't die easily. Jones twice tried to kill him with blunt instrument blows to the temple, then finally strangled him.

Jones dumped his victim in the bathtub, put his own wallet with social security card in the pocket of Ellis's trousers, and placed several personal items on the body, including his pinkie ring and a gold chain given to him by his girlfriend. Then he poured gasoline over Ellis and set him afire. Jones hoped that police would think it was him when they found the burned body with his identification on it.

He made one terrible mistake. He didn't think to put the stopper in the bathtub, and most of the gasoline ran down the drain. Ellis' body was charred but not burned beyond recognition. His facial features were still intact. That, plus fingerprint evidence, told investigators that this body was not that of Ben Wiley Jones, Jr.

Jones was arrested four months later in Los Angeles, California, and brought back to Oklahoma to stand trial. Trial began April 18, 1974.

This case was the state's first trial under a new murder statute that concerned the killing of a person under seventeen years of age.

Jones' attorney, Don Manners, asked that the first degree murder charge be reduced to murder in the second degree, arguing that Jones' specific charge did not fall under the category of first degree murder.

I denied the motion. In a written opinion, I stated that a careful reading of the statute convinced me that "the legislature is saying that if you kill a child under seventeen while willfully or maliciously beating, injuring of using unreasonable force, you are guilty of murder in the first degree."

Earlier in the trial, I allowed prosecuting attorney Duane Miller to put on testimony from witnesses regarding Jones' robbery charge. Under normal circumstances, testimony about former crimes may not be admitted as evidence. However, I allowed Miller to use the charge since the prosecution considered it as motive for the killing. The prosecution argued that Jones killed Ellis to avoid going to prison for a robbery charge to which he had already pled guilty.

The jury returned a verdict of guilty after four-and-a-half hours of deliberation. Jones was sentenced to die in the execution chamber.

§ § §

15

Witness for the Prosecution

After more than a third of a century in the courtroom as a prosecutor, defense attorney, and judge, I found myself on the other side of the justice system--that of a witness. And like most people called to provide testimony, I never expected that I would become entangled in a crime.

Facts. About four o'clock on the morning of September 23, 1984, I was awakened by a telephone call. It was Kenneth Bechtel, a fellow whom I knew only casually. My personal relationship with Ken was pretty much limited to the fact that we were boating enthusiasts who kept our boats at Applegate Cove Marina in Sallisaw, Oklahoma.

Ken was in his mid fifties, had a full head of red hair, and was a fun guy to be around. I knew he was some kind of an executive with an oil company and lived in a nice home in Edmond, Oklahoma, although I had never been to his home. His wife's name was Donna.

Ken said he was at the Nichols Hills jail. His speech was slurred and hard to understand. "They tell me if I can get a responsible citizen to come down here and drive me home, I won't have to stay in jail all weekend. Can you come down here and agree to take me home?"

As a judge, I could have gone to the police station to bond him out. I had done that a lot of times during my thirteen years on the bench. But I had a policy that I wouldn't do it for drunks until they sobered up. I simply would not get a drunk out of jail and turn him loose on the street again.

I told Ken, "Put the police on the phone."

Officer Larry van Schuyver came on the line. The first question I asked him was, "Is Ken Bechtel still drunk?"

"Yeah, he's drunker than hell."

"Well, I'm not going to bond him out. I'm not going to set a bond and turn him loose."

Officer van Schuyver explained, "You don't have to do that. We'll turn him over to you if you agree to take him home and see that he gets inside the house...not leave him out on the street somewhere."

"Okay," I said. "I can do that."

Accordingly, I got dressed and drove over to the Nichols Hills police station. Ken Bechtel was "knee-walking drunk." That's a term I often used to describe a person so drunk he can't stand up unless helped.

The police told me Ken had spent the evening at a vintage wine-tasting party at the home of trucking magnate Jack Hodges. They found him at 3:15 a.m. parked at a major intersection, the engine running, and himself slumped over the steering wheel asleep. This was early on a Saturday morning. Rather than jail him on a drunkenness charge and hold him there until Monday when a municipal judge would set bail, they agreed to turn him over to me.

I had no idea where Bechtel lived. I only knew it was somewhere in Edmond. He was too drunk to give good directions. We drove around the section of town where he thought he lived for a half-hour or so until he spotted a street that looked familiar. We found his house.

By now, the hour was approaching five a.m. It was still dark. I rang the doorbell. A woman in a bathrobe opened the inner door; we spoke as best we could through the glass storm door. I thought at first it was Donna Bechtel. But it turned out to be a friend of Donna's named Billie who was visiting from Illinois.

I told her who I was and said I was bringing Ken home, that

Ken was so drunk he couldn't hit the ground with his hat.

"Where's Ken?" she asked.

I looked around. Ken wasn't there. He had gone around the side of the house to relieve himself.

When Ken came back, she let him in. "Hi, Billie," he said as he walked past her.

I turned, walked back to my car, drove home, and went back to bed--my Good Samaritan deed done for the day. Or so I thought.

Several hours later, Caroline and I were sitting at the breakfast table reading the newspaper and sipping coffee when the telephone rang. It was an Edmond police lieutenant.

"Did you take Kenneth Bechtel home last night?" he asked.

"Yes, I did. After talking to the Nichols Hills police, I drove him home and put him in his house."

He said, "Well, Ken Bechtel is dead. Donna Bechtel shot him about an hour ago."

"My God," I exclaimed.

The lieutenant asked, "Would you come down here and give us a complete statement of what you did and what Ken did, and all that?"

"Sure I will," I said. I drove to the Edmond police station and gave my statement.

Trial. District Attorney Bob Macy subpoenaed me to appear as a witness in the trial of Donna Lee Bechtel. I, of course, had to obey the subpoena. Testimony began April 10, 1985, Judge Leamon Freeman presiding.

Pat Williams was Donna Bechtel's attorney. His defense was that Donna acted in self-defense when she fatally shot her husband, even though he was asleep in their bedroom at the time.

A variety of women's groups took up Donna Bechtel's cause as a battered wife.

My direct testimony largely recounted the events of the morning of September 23. I told the jury about my call from Ken Bechtel, talking with the Nichols Hills police about his condition, driving him home, being met by a woman guest, and seeing that

Ken actually entered the house with the door closed behind him. Questioning was by Bob Macy.

Q: Your Honor, in these actions that you took on that particular night, were you acting in your official capacity or as a private citizen?

A: I was acting as a friend of Ken and Donna Bechtel to go get him and bring him home because I wouldn't have acted as an official in that situation because he was still very drunk. I wouldn't have bonded him out. You know, I could have done, because of his condition. I wouldn't have done that.

Q: At the time the Nichols Hills police released him to you, did they advise you of anything?

A: Yeah. They had his car impounded. That's why we had to ring the doorbell, the car keys. They said he could come get his car on Monday.

Q: Did they advise you of anything with respect to releasing him to you?

A: They said they had a policy that they would release somebody like that to a responsible citizen instead of having him stay in jail all night.

MR. MACY: No further questions.

Under cross-examination, defense attorney Pat Williams sought to make it seem as if I was somehow at fault. That is, if I had not intervened with the Nichols Hills police and driven Ken home, he would not have been shot, and Donna would not have been charged with his murder. Williams sought to hang that albatross around my neck in one prickly exchange that was more of an accusation than a question.

Q: But at any rate, he didn't stay in jail; not because he posted bond, but because he was allowed to leave the jail because you, Joe Cannon, came and got him and agreed to take him home and they released him for that reason?

MR. FARBER: Objection, your Honor.

THE COURT: Sustained.

Donna Bechtel, 49, took the stand in her own defense. In a full day of testimony, she told a history of her stormy marriage to Kenneth Bechtel. Frequently sobbing, she portrayed her husband as a man with a serious drinking problem who vented his frustrations on his wife. She testified she endured continuing physical abuse at his hands.

Bob Macy called me back as a rebuttal witness on the last day of trial. Over the objections of defense attorney Pat Williams, I told of a conversation with Peggy Harter, a friend of Donna Bechtel. The conversation took place about a month or six weeks after the slaying.

I testified to what Peggy told me. She said that Donna said some time before the slaying "that if Ken Bechtel ever hit her again, she'd kill him."

On the stand, Peggy Harter told a different story. She said she told me Donna Bechtel "should have" shot her husband...not that she actually threatened to do so.

But my memory was clear. I told attorney Pat Williams, "She didn't say that. She said what I said a minute ago."

Pat Williams delivered an emotional closing argument. He said it irked him that friends and relatives of the slain oilman who testified for the prosecution had said they did not notice his drinking problem. (I assume that included me.) He also criticized lawyers with a "button-down mentality" who didn't know whether the woman's religion prohibited divorce or not.

District Attorney Bob Macy, in his closing statement, asked why Donna Bechtel did not leave her husband instead of killing him. "There's no religion I know that says a woman can't leave a husband that batters her."

The seven-man, five-woman jury deliberated nearly five hours before finding Donna Bechtel guilty of murder in the first degree. She was sentenced to life in prison.

In handing down his sentence, Judge Leamon Freeman told the women's groups supporting Bechtel, "I share the concerns of the ladies groups...But ladies, you have selected the wrong case to use in publicizing the plight of battered wives."

A macabre joke got started around the courthouse. "If you get drunk and land in jail, don't call Judge Cannon to get you out. It might be fatal."

Epilogue #1. Immediately after her trial, Donna Bechtel's case gained national attention from women's groups. They rallied behind her as an example of how the justice system mistreats battered women.

Bechtel's conviction was overturned in June 1987 by Oklahoma's Court of Criminal Appeals. The court ruled she had been denied a fair trial when Judge Freeman refused to let a witness testify as to whether Donna was competent to waive her Miranda rights when first questioned by police. The opinion said a friend of Bechtel's who was staying with the couple the night of the slaying should have been allowed to give her opinion.

The new trial was set for April 1988 under a new judge and a new defense attorney. District Judge Richard Freeman presided over the second trial, and Garland A. Isaacs was hired to defend Donna.

Isaacs sought to subpoena secret records from my personnel file. He claimed, "The jury is entitled to know...what motive some witness might...color his testimony in a way that's adverse to the accused."

Judge Freeman refused the request, telling Isaacs, "You're just fishing, really, aren't you?"

Outside the presence of the jurors, Judge Freeman heard arguments about whether Denver psychologist Lenore Walker should be allowed to testify as an expert on "battered women syndrome." She said one of the myths about battered women is "that they could just leave if they wanted to." Walker, who had studied more than 2,000 battered women, said that women who suffer from the syndrome develop a "learned helplessness."

Assistant District Attorney Fern Smith objected to the inclusion of this testimony, saying that Donna Bechtel had "systematically educated herself" since the first trial and had changed her story on the theory to better portray herself as a battered woman.

Further doubt was thrown on the value of such testimony when a Kansas psychiatrist hired by the prosecution told the judge that "Battered Wife Syndrome" is not recognized as a legitimate diagnosis among psychiatrists.

The hearing ended with Judge Freeman's ruling against allowing the testimony.

Trial resumed, and Donna Lee Bechtel was again found guilty. Jurors stated that she had other options besides shooting her husband, and the physical evidence did not support her testimony that he had beaten her.

For a second time, Donna Lee Bechtel was led out of the courtroom to face a life in prison.

Epilogue #2. In a landmark ruling, the Oklahoma Court of Criminal Appeals in September 1992 granted a third trial to Donna Lee Bechtel. The court overturned her conviction on the grounds that testimony on battered women's syndrome was not allowed during her trial.

Six weeks later, saying she could not face the ordeal of yet a third trial, Donna pleaded guilty to a lesser charge of manslaughter. Her sentence was commuted to time served.

On October 13, 1992, Donna Lee Bechtel walked out of the courtroom a free person.

§ § §

16

Ruminating in Retirement

One of the privileges of growing old is the freedom to reminisce on life's experiences and offer commentary on what may lie ahead. The joy of reminiscing lies in our ability to, in the words of the poet, "take from the altars of the past, not the ashes but the embers."

I've always liked the question Socrates asked of an old friend at the beginning of Plato's *The Republic*. Socrates said, "What I enjoy most is talking with men who are really old. It seems right to inquire of them, as if they had traveled a long journey which we perhaps will have to travel, to ask what is the journey like, rough and difficult, or easygoing and smooth?"

His friend answered, "There is only one reason for what happens; not old age, but the man's character."

In this vein, then, I offer the following opinions and observations as being the product of my reflecting on fifty years of experience in the criminal justice system as a trial attorney, district attorney, defense lawyer, and trial judge.

Making Sense of Sentencing

My conduct on the bench earned me the reputation of being a "law and order" judge. That's because I tended to be rather hard on confirmed criminals.

Most Americans are skeptical of their criminal justice system. They think the courts are too lenient with criminals. Mr. Average Citizen, in every survey I've seen, would mete out sentences approximately three times longer than criminals actually serve.

I used to fight the Department of Corrections all the time about paroling people. Time and again they would parole someone, and he'd hardly be back on the street before he was committing another crime. In fact, I've joked, "We're getting to the point where the criminal will be out of prison and back home again before the sheriff who delivered him there gets back to his own office."

Philosophy

Scholars list three competing and sometimes overlapping philosophies of sentencing--rehabilitation, punishment, and incarceration. We all tend to be guided by one of these three principles more than the others. That's also true for state legislators who set the sentencing guidelines.

Rehabilitation. I was never strong on rehabilitation because I don't believe you can rehabilitate a hardened criminal.

Back in the 1950s and 1960s, states made rehabilitation rather than punishment the central principal. Parole boards began assessing the prisoner's fitness for release, not whether he had suffered punishment commensurate with his crime.

In my experience, some kinds of crooks never get rehabilitated. If they are a thief, they're out stealing again as soon as they're back on the street. Child molesters are the worst when it comes to being repeat offenders. That's why I was pretty hard on people who molested children.

I used to tell a story in my speeches. Halfway between Oklahoma City and the prison at McAlester, there is a house that is known as "God's House." When the guards deliver a convicted killer down to the prison, they often stop off at the God's house. Prisoners know that this is their last hope--they have been turned down too many times by the parole board, and suddenly they have "found God."

"Finding God" seems to work. That's one of the things they always try. I predict that Glen Burton Ake, as bad as he is, will wind up some day saying he's found God.

That's when the preachers move in. As soon as a criminal says he's found God, there's a whole bunch of preachers that will try to come to his rescue. They start lobbying to get him paroled. I don't know why, they just do.

They get these preachers to working on their behalf; organizing protests and getting people to write letters; finding people who know them and will tell the parole board they're good people, have been rehabilitated, won't do it again, and all that good stuff.

Preachers ought to stay in the pulpit, and stay out of politics.

Punishment. "Let the punishment fit the crime," people say. Few would argue with the idea that the criminal should suffer punishment commensurate with his crime. That sounds good on paper, but it rarely works out in the real world.

For one thing, some crimes are so heinous that to subject the criminal to commensurate punishment would be considered "cruel and inhuman treatment."

For another, sentencing guidelines are set by the state legislature. Burglary gets two to five years, second degree manslaughter is four years to life, and so forth. I think the sentences on some crimes are far too short. After serving a third of his sentence, the Pardons and Parole Board has to give a criminal a parole hearing. This doesn't mean they have to grant him a parole, nonetheless he is eligible for one.

The argument of cost doesn't stand up. A legislature never has enough money to fund all the programs it wants to, yet only 3.3 percent of government spending in Oklahoma is devoted to building and operating our prison system. This is far less than what is spent on education and social welfare.

I'd like to ask, what better welfare is there than the safety and security of one's person and sanctity of one's home?

Incarceration. In principle, I am mostly oriented towards incarceration. I want to keep the criminals off the street. If a criminal is behind bars, he's not out committing other crimes.

That's why I sentenced Johnnie Allen Muse in 1981 to three life terms for a series of armed convenience-store robberies. I said in making the ruling, "I thought it was time he be locked up for good before he kills somebody.''

Similarly, I gave Kevin Michael Estell five life sentences in 1985 for two Heritage Hills burglaries and attacking an elderly man and his daughter. The sentences were to run consecutively, which meant he would never get out of prison. ''His actions had shown there was no chance of his ever being rehabilitated and that the only solution was for Estell to be separated from society,'' I said.

Intermediate Offenders Act

In 1983, the state legislature passed a new law called the Nonviolent Intermediate Offender Act which was to go into effect January 1, 1984.

The law greatly expanded the role of personnel in the Department of Corrections in sentencing young non-violent offenders. If the offender is placed on probation and subsequently violates it, it would be solely up to the Department of Corrections--not a judge--to decide whether he should be placed in prison.

The minute I read the law, I knew it was unconstitutional. But I couldn't just willy-nilly, out of the blue, declare a statute unconstitutional. A judge has to have the issue come before him in a case before he can render an opinion.

My opportunity came in October 1985. It happened to be my turn to serve as chief criminal judge, the person who assigns criminal cases. I spotted a suit filed by Bob Ravitz in the public defender's office. It was filed on behalf of a client who said his constitutional rights had been violated by corrections officials when they revoked his probation without benefit of a court hearing. I immediately assigned the case to myself.

I ruled that the process was unconstitutional. After hearing a description of the administrative procedure, I said, ''This would make the founders of the Constitution turn over in their graves if they were sitting here today.'' I barred corrections officials from incarcerating inmates under the act unless they were granted court hearings.

My ruling was appealed, of course. But in June 1986 it was upheld by Oklahoma's Court of Criminal Appeals, thus striking down the 1984 juvenile offenders act.

By this time, we had a mess on our hands. Approximately 150 juveniles at the correctional facility at Lexington were there under an unconstitutional statute. It also happened that I was now presiding judge for Oklahoma County, so it became my job to figure out a way to deal with the problem.

It wasn't practical to bring them all to the county courthouse. We didn't have room at the jail, nor enough guards and deputies, and so on. So instead of "Mohammed going to the mountain," so to speak, I decided to "move the mountain to Mohammed."

I moved the district court to Lexington for a day. The Department of Corrections provided a bus, I rounded up a dozen district judges, a bunch of deputies, court clerks, public defenders, and assistant district attorneys, and we all went down to Lexington. We met in the large lobby, each judge seated at a table with provisions for a court clerk, assistant district attorney, and public defender.

I explained to the prisoners why we were here. They had been convicted under an unconstitutional law, and they had three choices which they should talk over with their court-appointed attorney. The choices were:

1. Do nothing, and serve out their sentence.
2. Be taken back to Oklahoma County and have a new trial.
3. Plead guilty, and be sentenced to time served and released.

Only one defendant asked for a new trial.

It took us about fourteen hours to complete the task. We went home tired, but having the satisfaction of knowing we had solved a nearly impossible situation.

Death Penalty.

A reporter asked Judge Charles Owens if he thought the death penalty would keep people from killing again. Charlie alluded to a recently executed murderer in his answer. "Well, it sure will keep him from doing it."

'Nuff said.

Confusion. The U.S. Supreme Court really screwed things up in 1973 and 1976 when they threw out our death penalty laws. They didn't say the death penalty was illegal; rather, they said our laws regulating the death penalty were unconstitutional.

We spent the next ten years "jumping through hoops" in an effort to find some formula that would please the high court justices. We never knew what they liked, we only knew what they didn't like.

Each time an appeals court overturned a case, we found out one more thing we shouldn't have done, but we still did not know what we should do. Consider the case of Glen Burton Ake, for example. The high court ruled Ake had been denied a fair trial because he was not provided with court-appointed, state-funded psychiatric help. That had never been required before. The Supreme Court was making new law.

It's no wonder most citizens were unable to follow the bizarre legal twists of the criminal justice system.

Life or death, those were our only two options for a convicted killer. Only death didn't mean death, and life didn't mean life. My thirty years of dealing with Oklahoma's criminal justice system taught me that a life sentence usually turned out to be about eight years.

Life without parole. In 1986, a third option was created--life without the possibility of parole. Many people who had qualms about assigning the death penalty had been asking for this option. The people overwhelmingly approved this amendment to the state constitution which went into effect November 1, 1987.

The life-without-parole amendment had not been passed when Benito Jerome Bowie ordered the December 23, 1984, killing of Eric Douglas Dunn during a party.

Bowie was the head of a dope ring in Oklahoma City. Dunn had struck one of his employees in an altercation. Bowie ordered Dexter Tyrone McDade to kill Dunn and was present in the room when it happened.

The trial took place in April 1988. Bowie was found guilty of murder in the first degree. He got death.

The appeals court affirmed the murder conviction, but it reversed the punishment. Judge Lane wrote the opinion. He said they reversed the sentence on the grounds that my instructions to the jury did not include the option of life without parole.

Poppycock! We didn't have the life-without-parole law at the time Bowie killed Dunn. That amendment didn't go into effect until three years after the commission of the crime. Justice Lane was applying a 1987 law to a 1984 crime thereby making it, in effect, retroactive.

To apply a law retroactively is against the law. For example, if I were to come into your house and steal something of value, the law at the time I steal it is what governs what my punishment can be. You can't change it retroactively.

Some of the other justices wrote pretty powerful dissenting opinions, saying in effect, you can't do that. But Lane did it anyway.

Lane's opinion stood. The state did not appeal it to the Supreme Court.

Execution.

After twenty years of legal nit-picking and fuzzy-headed judicial decisions, an Oklahoma death penalty case finally made it through the Supreme Court. On September 10, 1990, Charles Troy Coleman became the first Oklahoma inmate to be executed in 24 years.

Coleman, 43, was convicted of the February 9, 1979, murders of John and Roxie Seward in Muskogee, Oklahoma. After eleven years of appeals, including seven to the U.S. Supreme Court, he finally met his fate.

Now the death penalty meant something.

Caring for Juries

The U.S. Constitution says we are entitled to have our case heard by a jury of our peers. This principle is ingrained in our culture. For the concept to work, however, people selected as jurors must be very conscientious about their duties.

I am a strong believer in the jury system. My experience over the past fifty years has shown that most jury members have taken their responsibilities very seriously.

In our system, the jury is the "trier of fact." Its job, after hearing all the evidence in the case, is to answer the question, "Did this person do what he is accused of doing?" The judge's role is the "interpreter of law." His job is to ensure that the law is followed in the conduct of the trial.

Pastoral care. I tended to be very solicitous of my juries. I looked after them almost as a pastoral charge. I'd tell them, "If there's anything you need, you just let me know. We're not all on the same schedule. If you have to use the restroom, just hold up your hand and we'll take a recess. We're not in any big hurry. Or if you need a drink of water, or anything like that, let us know."

The more a judge takes care of the jury, the more the jurors are going to listen to what he says the law is--whether they agree or not. Take a death penalty case, for example: the judge may be instructing the jury about the law in a death penalty case, and one juror may have some reservations about sentencing a person to death. But if a judge whom he trusts is talking about when they can give the death penalty, this trust may override their belief.

I could tell by the looks on their faces when they became confused. I might stop the trial and explain to the jurors what was happening here, what was going on. Other times, I might apologize to the jurors for delays in the proceedings.

Conscientious jurors. Because they're so conscientious and want to do the right thing, most jurors place a heavy burden on the judge. They think the judge knows everything there is to know about the lawsuit. In fact, he may have heard about the case five minutes before he said, "Call your first witness."

On the other hand, the lawyers may have had three months to study and prepare. The judge is picking it up as it goes, but he's trained to do that. However, if he appears not to know more than the lawyers, he's not doing his job.

The judge has to be really careful about his facial expressions, he can't laugh--unless something happens spontaneously that causes the whole courtroom to burst into laughter, in which case he can chuckle a little bit. I had one case, for example, where a guy said that it was a picture of his eye on the back of a one-dollar bill. It was such a ludicrous claim that everybody laughed. I always turned away from the jury when I knew I was about to snicker.

Juror accommodations. I tried a murder case in which the jury was sequestered, meaning it was "kept apart from public view" for the duration of the trial. Jurors were instructed to bring enough clothes and toiletries to last four days. They were put up in a downtown hotel.

My bailiff called me at home that first night. It was near midnight. He said conditions were awful--the rooms were dirty and cockroaches were running around like they owned the place--and the jurors were very upset.

I swore my wife in as an assistant bailiff and took her down there with me. I thought we might need a woman to help the female jurors get packed and out of their rooms.

I arranged for rooms at the Sheraton, then a new hotel, about four blocks away.

The police department was next on my list to call. I told the captain on duty, "I need about twenty police cars with drivers." He did as we asked.

The jurors were assembled in the lobby of the old hotel. I explained, "My bailiff told me that you all were complaining that the place was dirty, and there were cockroaches and stuff, so I have made arrangements to put you in the Sheraton Hotel.

Both sides of the street were lined with police cars, lights flashing. We had the jurors walk down the middle of the street between the lines of police cars. Since this was a murder case, I didn't want anybody to come anywhere near that jury except me or my bailiff. So it made for quite a parade.

The next morning, I spoke to Bob Martin, the court administrator. I told him, "Don't ever use that hotel again for a jury because it's not a fit place for nice people to stay in."

Jury shirkers. Forty-two prospective jurors failed to appear for jury duty on March 1, 1982. That got my dander up. I issued subpoenas for them to explain their absences or face charges of contempt.

No-shows create a real dilemma. On the one hand, the judge can send a sheriff out and arrest them, throw them in jail, and cite them for contempt. On the other hand, do we want that kind of a person on our jury--a person who doesn't have any more respect for the law than that? That's the dilemma.

Of those forty-two names on the list, only twelve showed up for the hearing March 19. After listening to their excuses, some of which were pretty weak, I said, "I could not find it in my heart to put any of you in jail."

Instead, I let them off with a lecture. "If citizens continue to shy away from jury duty, the courts will be forced to use skidrow bums and bring down old folks from the nursing home to serve as jurors." I asked, "Do you want your case decided by those kinds of people?"

Spousal recusal. I used to have a rule that I wouldn't let a woman sit on a jury whose husband was a lawyer. (Note: Lawyers themselves are forbidden by law to sit on a jury.) I'd say to the woman, "At the end of this trial, I'm going to instruct you as to what the law is. Are you going to give me your word that you're going to follow what I tell you the law is? Or are you going to ask your husband what he thinks the law is? You see, he's not in this trial, he doesn't have anything to do with it."

I might let them sit on a jury in a trial that was going to last less than one day. But I'd never let a woman go home and spend the night with her lawyer-husband and come back and continue being a juror. That was my own personal rule. Because I knew human nature.

Note taking. I didn't let jurors take notes. The reason was that one of them might be a secretary who could take shorthand. Then later in deliberating the case in the jury room, one juror might say, "So and so said this." The secretary might whip out her pad and say, "No, that isn't what he said. Here's what he said, and I can give it to you verbatim exactly what he said."

That puts other jurors at a disadvantage. So that's why I didn't do it.

Jury consultants. Beginning about twenty years ago, it became popular for lawyers to hire a new breed of experts, called "jury consultants," to help them pick jurors likely to be favorable to their case. The whole practice remains controversial.

I didn't like it. So I set some restrictions. If some lawyer wanted to hire an expert jury consultant, the consultant would have to sit in the back of the courtroom in the audience area. The lawyer could talk to him at recesses and go over things with him then. But I wouldn't let the consultant sit inside the bar at the counsel table where he could talk with the lawyer and give advice while *voir dire* was going on. I just wouldn't let them do it.

Juror enthusiasm. Back when I was Muskogee County Attorney, an exuberant juror almost caused me to lose an important case.

I was making my closing argument in a child molestation case. It was an awful crime. The child was very young. I was determined to put the molester away forever.

In those days, a lawyer could walk up and down in front of the jury rail while making his presentation. No longer. But that's what I was doing that day, walking up and down in front of the jury box. I got really wound up in my speech and fired off what I thought was a brilliant remark. A male juror in the front row evidently thought so too, for he jumped up, stuck out his hand, and exclaimed, "Well, I God damned sure agree with that!"

Without thinking, I reached out and shook hands with him. I shouldn't have done that. A lawyer is not permitted to shake hands with members of the jury.

Defense counsel immediately objected and asked for a mistrial. I apologized to the judge and explained that I didn't plan or mean to do that. It was just one of those things that happened under the spontaneity of the moment.

The judge thought it over for a minute, then overruled the motion.

Today, if that happened in my court, I would probably declare a mistrial.

Waiting on Witnesses

After having conducted thousands of trials, I could almost always tell when a witness was lying, especially alibi witnesses. These are the people who say, "Johnnie was with me the entire night of the murder." The vein in his or her neck starts throbbing.

Tangled webs. Alibi witnesses can't stand up to cross-examination unless they're telling the truth. They think they can make up a story, but the more they are cross-examined, the more twisted the story gets. Sir Walter Scott echoed this sentiment when he penned the well-known line, "O what a tangled web we weave, when first we practice to deceive."

I used to try to get district attorneys to prosecute alibi witnesses for perjury when it was as plain as the nose on their face that they were lying. But they didn't often do it.

Talking too much. The worst witnesses are the ones who try to answer more than was asked of them. When I was a practicing lawyer, I used to lecture my witnesses before trial. It didn't do any good. I'd say, "Don't answer or volunteer anything unless I ask you. Just answer what I ask you. And when the other lawyer gets up, for God's sakes don't do it because he's trying to trap you. So don't *ever* add anything extra to what he's asking you."

Opening the door. Lay witnesses don't understand courtroom rules. There are lots of things a witness can't be asked on cross-examination unless the other side first opens the subject--what lawyers call "opening the door." And if your witness opens the door by volunteering some piece of information, it gives the other side the opportunity to cross-examine him on that matter.

For example, the witness might say, "Johnnie is really a nice fellow. He's never been in trouble with the law in his whole life." But suppose Johnnie has a rap sheet as long as his arm. Now the other side has a right to go into that whole rap sheet.

I used to tell them, "Keep your answer short and sweet. Don't open the door to things you don't want to have brought out."

Looking all around. I used to instruct witnesses, "Look at the jury. Don't be looking all around. And don't ever look at your lawyer when being questioned by the opposing side."

A lot of times, if a witness is asked a question that's potentially damaging, they'll look over at their lawyer at the counsel table, seeking some sign whether to answer yes or no. They do that because they've been asked a question that they weren't prepared to answer.

When I was a judge and saw that behavior, I'd stop the trial and call the lawyer to the bench. I'd tell him, "If you nod a yes or no answer to your witness, I'll hold you in contempt."

In my days as a trial lawyer, if a witness did that to me I'd say, "Don't look at your lawyer. Look at me." I did that to call it to the attention of the jury.

Losing one's cool. Another instruction I gave witnesses was, "Never get mad. That's what cross-examiners try to do, get under your skin." I said, "If they make you mad, you've lost and they've won."

TV in the courtroom. I debated Ralph Hodges, then chief justice of the Oklahoma Supreme Court, on the topic of allowing live television in the courtroom. I spoke out strongly against it. It causes witnesses to say too much. They don't want to appear stupid or ignorant in front of a television audience, so they find it hard to say simply, "I'm not sure about that," or "I don't know."

The television camera makes actors out of everybody. It makes them want to show off how smart they are. Again, it invites witnesses to do the number one thing they do wrong, which is to answer questions they weren't asked.

I've seen jury members roll their eyes when somebody gives some crazy, absolute lie. They would look off into space, or turn towards each other, as if to say, "Golly, did you hear what he said?"

Expert witnesses. These people are trained to testify. And the lawyer who takes one of them on and tries to cross him up is a damned fool.

I tried a big medical malpractice case one time involving claims of several million dollars. A big law firm was defending it. The lawyers were in my chambers getting ready to go out and start the cross-examination of the plaintiff's expert witness. He was a doctor, an OBGYN, board certified, diplomas from almost every major school, credentials coming out the wazoo, and recognized as one of the leading experts in town.

The lady lawyer who was assisting in the defense was slated to conduct the cross-examination. She boasted, "I'm going to go out there and tear him to pieces." Prior to law school, she had worked as a medical technician, and I guess she thought she knew everything. The lead attorney, her boss, pleaded, "Please, just go out there and keep your mouth shut."

She tried. But the more she talked, the worse it got. By the time she got through, the doctor had torn her completely to pieces.

When we got back in my chambers, she said, "I tore him up, didn't I?"

Her boss and I looked at each other, like, "Oh, Gawd. You've gotta be kidding!" She thought she'd really done something wonderful.

Lecturing the Lawyers

You can't teach lawyers to be trial lawyers. That's a quality they're born with. Like champion golfer Tiger Woods, it's a gift from God.

I have always been a big believer in the notion that trial lawyers are not taught to be trial lawyers in law school. How to be a good trial lawyer is not something found in textbooks. Trial lawyers are born, not taught. They can improve their skills and get better with practice. But the basic talent is something they got here with. You can't teach them the right tone and inflection or the right timing. You can't teach them when to talk and when to sit down and shut up.

In my lectures to young lawyers and at law school, I have tried to teach them that just as everyone can't be a brain surgeon, so also everyone can't be a trial lawyer.

It's hard to explain, because it's a feeling inside you. You know how to do it. You're confident. You know what you're doing. Better than that, you know you know what you're doing.

Mental agility. What makes a good trial lawyer? Number one, you've got to be really quick on your feet.

You've got to be well-educated. You have to be able to know what the case is *really* about.

Feeling. You've got to have a natural feeling for the person and the surroundings--the jurors and the witnesses, as well as who the judge is and how far he's going to let you go.

Good lawyers know how much rein a judge is going to give them in asking questions. You don't want to let yourself get in a position where you're being overruled all the time. That makes the jury wonder about your competency. If every time you stand up and object, and the judge overrules you, jurors tend to think, "That lawyer must not be too good. The judge overrules him every time he opens his mouth."

Human relations. A trial lawyer has to be a real, board-certified, human nature expert. He has to know what makes people tick. Take my case of the lemon-spotted coon dog, for example (Chap. 1). When I heard that old farmer mention he was looking for his lemon-spotted coon dog, instinctively I thought, "Hell, the jury will buy that."

There are certain things in life that everybody does. If you can get the jurors going with you on things you know about, you can get them to stay with you on matters less understandable. And you can tell by looking at the jury whether they're getting it or not. If they start counting the ceiling tiles, you'd better switch subjects...because they aren't listening.

You've got to form a bond between you and the jury. They have to have a "feeling" for you, and you've got to create that feeling. (Of course, you don't have to bond to the point where they stand up and shake hands with you.)

Details. You've got to be able to delve into the little things. The little things are what prove a lawsuit. A witness might say, "I went to town yesterday." The rebuttal witness might say, "No he didn't." Who is telling the truth? It's the details of what the witness did that makes it true or not true. If he can't answer any details, he's probably not telling the truth. "Well, what time did you leave?" "Oh, I don't know...."

You've got to know how to work things around and what questions to ask, and when to let it go. And don't browbeat the witness.

Pride. Most good trial lawyers are doing it for themselves, not their client. It's pride in what they're doing that drives them to win cases. The client is the beneficiary, but the lawyer wants the victory. That's what you want if you want to be a good trial lawyer.

Honesty. You can't succeed as a trial lawyer, and remain a good trial lawyer, if you're not totally, completely honest with the judge. Judges form opinions about whether they can take a lawyer's word for something. After I had been on the bench a few years, I could name a whole list of lawyers of whom I wouldn't believe a damned word they said. The judge has to have confidence in you. And that confidence will spread to the jury and help you to bond with them.

Brevity. So many lawyers just talk and talk and talk and don't make any sense. They need to simplify. They've got to come off of being a legal scholar and down to being a regular lawyer. As Sam Ervin, chairman of the Senate Watergate Committee, used to say, "I'm just a country lawyer." Baloney! He was a great legal scholar; he just had the ability to bring the legal jargon down to the level of Mr. Average Citizen.

I've told many a lawyer in a non-jury trial, where I'd heard all the facts and knew the rebuttal argument wasn't going to add anything, "You don't want to make a closing rebuttal argument do you?"

"Oh, yes I do, Judge."

"Well, I already had my mind made up to rule in your favor, but I'll bet you that you can think of some reason why I shouldn't. So why don't you try? Go ahead with what you want to say."

"Oh, I've changed my mind, Judge."

Terminal ability. Know when to quit. Many times a novice lawyer will ask a witness, "Did you go to the railroad station last Saturday before this thing happened?" The witness will say, "Yes." He'll say, "Did you say you went to the railroad station last Saturday?"

As a judge, I couldn't resist the temptation to say, "The witness has already answered that question. He told you 'yes.'"

Those kinds of things make a lawyer look bad in front of the jury. If you make a good point, you don't have to have it repeated two or three times. You've got a closing argument you can use it in.

I used to lecture young lawyers at Oklahoma University Law School, "If you've got something important to say, say it. Then shut up and sit down.

§ § §

17

Epilogue

I retired from the bench in September 1988 for medical reasons. I was a diabetic. My health was getting so bad my doctors convinced me that undergoing the stress of another major trial could be life-threatening.

Andy Coats, now dean of the OU Law School but then an outstanding trial attorney, paid me a nice tribute when my retirement was announced. Andy said, "It's a sad day for the Oklahoma County judiciary. We've lost a great judge."

My record on the bench is one to be proud of. I tried the first DNA case in Oklahoma, the first blood spatter case, the first bite marks case, the first comparative negligence case, and the first atomic energy explosion case. During my last term, I tried sixty-one murder cases in which the state was asking for the death penalty, of which 57 resulted in convictions. All 57 of those guilty verdicts were appealed to the Oklahoma Court of Criminal Appeals, and most were appealed to the U.S. Supreme Court. All were upheld except one. In that one case, the punishment phase--but not the guilty verdict itself--was reversed.

Retirement to Florida

Our new home was to be a fifty-foot trawler, twin-diesel, deep-water boat. Years before, I had made a down payment on the boat, and it was fully paid for by the time I retired. It had a front cabin with two beds, a big wheelhouse cabin, large galley (kitchen), refrigerator, ice-maker, and central heat and air.

Caroline and I took the boat, just the two of us, from Sallisaw, down the Arkansas, down the White, into the Mississippi, on to New Orleans, and across the Gulf to Destin, Florida. We planned to stop in Destin for not more than a week, then continue on south to somewhere in the Florida Keys. But we liked it so well there in Destin that we decided to stay. I joined the Burnt Pines Country Club and arranged to keep my boat at the club's marina. We lived on the boat.

Stroke and heart attack. Although I didn't know it at the time, I suffered both a stroke and a heart attack.

I was standing on the first tee at the Burnt Pines Country Club with my regular playing group, getting ready to hit our drives. I did something unusual--at least for me. I whiffed the ball. Missed it completely! I swung again, and whiffed it again. For a five-handicap golfer, that was pretty bad.

I turned to my playing partners, "Fellows, I've got to leave you. Somebody's got to drive me home, because something is not right."

The doctors told me I had a brain-stem stroke. It didn't affect cognition or speech, but it upset my equilibrium and balance and it impaired muscle coordination. I didn't learn about the heart attack until later.

I told Caroline, "We're going to go back to Oklahoma City." We arrived shortly before Christmas.

To tell the truth, I thought I was dying. I thought that that Christmas was going to be my last Christmas, and I really wanted to see my kids and grandkids before I went.

Dr. Charles Bethea is one of the best cardiologists in this part of the country. My daughter, who is a medical technician, got me in to see him. Thank God. Dr. Bethea saved my life. He called in Dr. James Hartsuck, cardiology surgeon, to do triple bypass. He said, "You'd already fallen over a cliff, and I threw you a rope."

Caroline cared for me night and day for nine months. She did the heavy work, kept house, saw to my medications, and gave me my shots. Many nights she didn't get any sleep at all. If it weren't for her, I wouldn't be alive and writing these thoughts.

Looming blindness. When we got back to Florida, my vision continued to worsen. I was going blind, and the doctors down there couldn't figure out what to do. By 1992, it had gotten so bad I called to Dr. Tom Acers in Oklahoma City. He said, "You need to talk to Pat Wilkinson."

I had been treated by Dr. C.P. "Pat" Wilkinson during his years at the Dean McGee Eye Institute in Oklahoma City. He had recently moved to Baltimore as head of ophthalmology at Johns Hopkins University. I told him I was about to go blind. "Can I come up to Johns Hopkins and see if there is anything you can do to help me?" I asked.

He said, "Judge, I'd be glad to take care of you. But there's a guy at Emory University in Atlanta who knows more about it than anybody in the whole world. He's a lot closer to you there than I am here in Baltimore."

That's how I got connected with Dr. Aaberg, whom I credit with saving my eyesight. He explained that diabetes causes the ends of blood vessels in the eyes to bleed. He had to seal those ends. They use lasers to do that. So for the next fifteen weeks, Caroline made the six-hour drive to Atlanta for my treatments. During that time, Dr.Aaberg gave me over a thousand laser zaps in both eyes.

Judging the Judges

Throughout much of 1995, I was gravely ill and bed-bound. The doctors couldn't figure out what was wrong. I couldn't even get off the boat.

With little else to break the monotony, I watched the O.J. Simpson trial on television. That broke one of my cardinal rules of never watching televised trials because they're so poorly done. But I was hard-pressed for something to occupy my mind.

What I saw absolutely infuriated me. I stayed glued to the set, not because I thought it so good, but because I couldn't believe it could be so bad. It prompted me to start an angry letter of complaint to the Florida Bar Association, a letter that never got finished...until now.

Judicial incompetence. I wanted to tell them that Lance Ito was absolutely the worst judge I had ever seen. He made rulings that made no legal sense whatever. His conduct of that trial was a disgrace to the legal system. I would have told them that Ito was no more capable as a judge than I would have been as an Apollo astronaut.

Unfortunately, the O.J. trial--or some part of it--was watched by almost every single living American. This proceeding made a lasting impression on the psyche of America.

I would have issued a disclaimer, namely, that I do not take issue with the jury's verdict. They heard the evidence, they deliberated, and they made a decision. That's good enough for me.

What I am exercised about is the manner in which the O.J. trial was conducted. There was nothing about the trial that resembled a real trial. It was broadcast on live television all over the United States. Ito himself was constantly playing to the television cameras.

Ito lost control of the courtroom on the first day and never regained it. Johnny Cochran, his former boss in the DA's office, ran that courtroom.

About half of Ito's rulings were wrong. Some were major rulings. If there was any saving grace it was that about half of his bad rulings favored the prosecution and half favored the defense. In other words, he was an equal-opportunity bumbler.

He sat on his backside and let the defense make a whipping boy out of Detective Mark Fuhrman. Nothing that Detective Fuhrman did was illegal or wrong and, as a matter of fact, his cross-examination had little to do with who killed Nicole Simpson and Ronald Goldman. Rather, the cross-examiner focused mainly on whether he was a racist.

F. Lee Bailey was the person who turned the trial into a racist nightmare. Ito allowed him to do it. Whether Fuhrman used the ''N'' word once or a thousand times, it didn't prove who killed those two young people. Whether you believe the use of the ''N'' word is good or bad, it had nothing to do with establishing the guilt or innocence of O.J. Simpson.

The national media portrayed F. Lee Bailey as one of the great lawyers of our time. It's always been a mystery to me how such reputations are acquired. Some lawyers, like Bailey, seem to lose almost every important case and still end up with a reputation as a good lawyer. Despite Mr. Bailey's carefully cultivated reputation, however, he has repeatedly been in trouble with the law in both federal and state courts.

Another thing Ito did wrong was to let the defense put on experts to testify that the L.A. crime lab *could* have contaminated the DNA samples, not that they did. It was purely hypothetical speculation, yet Ito let the defense put it on as evidence.

This leads me to pose a question to the judges who are reading this: Can you in your wildest imagination see yourself opening court with a blanket invitation to lawyers, "Do you have anything to say?" Would you let them babble on about the television talk show they watched the previous night in which guests offered comments about this case? Well, Ito did.

Ito held more bench conferences ("sidebars," they called them) in this one trial than I held in the nearly twenty years I served on the bench. Any good judge knows what to rule as soon as one side objects, and he usually knows what the objection is going to be before it is made. He has probably ruled on the same objection hundreds of times before.

I think I could have tried the O.J. case in about three weeks. What's more, I could name at least a dozen other judges in my city who could have done the same thing.

TV experts. The talk shows were nightly fare at my sickbed. Most of the so-called experts didn't know what they were talking about. All were biased either strongly in favor of O.J., or strongly against him. I reckon it's required of a TV guest to be a vocal advocate for one side or the other. There's no room in television for the voice of moderation. The medium thrives on controversy and it hates objective, rational and measured analysis.

My particular dislike was Gerry Spence, the Buffalo Man. He always showed up wearing a fringed, buckskin coat. The national media hailed him as one of the country's great lawyers, but I never figured out why. I never could decide whether he was hustling for law business or auditioning for a movie role. The sheepskin clothes looked like something borrowed from Fess Parker, star of the "Daniel Boone" television series. I wonder if he ever returned them.

We have a lot of good hardworking judges in this country--judges who know the law and know how to try a case. Unfortunately, those are not the ones we see on television.

Selection of judges. On the whole, the United States has the finest judicial system in the world--Lance Ito not withstanding. But that doesn't mean we can't make it better.

One thing I would change is the manner in which judges are named. My native Oklahoma, as do many other states, has a hybrid system for picking judges. District judges are elected by the people on a nonpartisan ballot, and appellate judges are appointed by the governor from a slate proposed by a judicial nominating committee for a six-year term but run for reelection on a retention ballot. If I were to conduct a survey as to whether judges should be elected or appointed, I suspect the public would be about equally divided on that issue.

My opinion is that if people have enough sense to vote for whom they want to be President of the United States, they ought also to have enough sense to vote for the person they want to be judge. This includes appellate as well as district judges.

Judges should represent the people they judge. They should understand their constituents' hopes, aspirations and dreams. They should understand how their constituents think, work and live. And the incompetent judges should be removable from office by a free and open election of the people.

In the thirty or so years since Oklahoma has had the retention ballot for supreme court justices, no one has ever *not* been retained. Hence, it amounts to a lifetime appointment.

Choosing a chief justice. Another thing I would change is the selection process for the chief justice of the state supreme court. My feeling is that the chief justice ought to be elected by his peers. At present, Oklahoma rotates that assignment every two years by seniority. This procedure doesn't always assure the best-qualified person will occupy that seat of great influence and power.

In my opinion, the person chosen to be chief justice should not only be the most learned in the law, but he should also meet the common sense and compassion tests.

Moreover, switching the chief justice around is not an efficient way to do things. I know a lot of my fellow judges agree with me.

Oklahoma's Supreme Court scandal. Back in the 1960s, Oklahoma had a big scandal in its supreme court. Two justices went to jail, one was impeached, and a powerful legal family was toppled.

Earl Welch was the acknowledged dean of the court. His name gave rise to the so-called "Welch Fix," a scam that guaranteed a steady stream of income for Justice Welch and two of his colleagues, Justice N.S. Corn and Justice N.B. Johnson.

The scam was cleverly contrived and difficult to trace. For example, a lawyer involved in a big money case might ask the local judge to disqualify himself. If the judge refused to recuse, the lawyer would then appeal to the state supreme court. Welch would see to it that the local judge was disqualified and a crony judge named who would make a favorable ruling. Naturally, payoff monies would mysteriously find their way into Welch's secret cache and the crony judge's pocket.

It took the courage of William A. Berry, then the junior justice on the court, and G.T. Blankenship, then a state legislator, to expose the ring. (Note: See *Justice for Sale,* by Berry and Alexander.) Welch and Corn were convicted of tax evasion, and Johnson was impeached.

It was then that the retention ballot was brought in as an attempt to reform the system. I think that was a mistake. I believe that any qualified lawyer ought to be able to run for any judicial office.

Oh, were I but twenty years younger, what great things I would attempt for my beloved Oklahoma!

Becoming a believer

Throughout most of my life, I had been a borderline believer. To paraphrase Voltaire, God and I had a nodding acquaintance, but we never spoke. Not any more. I am convinced that God spared me for a purpose and a reason. And that purpose is for me to finish this book.

Caroline and I moved back to Oklahoma City in January 1998. I applied for a change from medically retired to retired. That status was granted by the Court of the Judiciary in October 1999. Subsequently, I asked the supreme court to change my status from inactive retired to active retired. That status would make me eligible to help out judicial districts that needed more judges to handle cases. They turned me down. Nonetheless, I plan to continue seeking active retired status.

Time for tributes

Finally, I want to pay tribute to the people who helped me in researching cases and providing historical information. I wish to offer thanks to Burke Bailey, Irven Box, Bob Burke, Donna Deming, Drew Edmondson, Tommy Ferguson, Gene Frusher, J. Leland Gourley, Vinita Hoover, Perry Kaufman, Don Manners, Bob Martin, Richard Mask, Earl Mills, John Norman, Patricia Presley, Richard Wintory, and Charles Yadon.

The Hon. James Edmondson, one of my main helpers, has read and commented on the manuscript in its entirety. He had to fill the shoes of his dad and uncle. Bob Ravitz did research above and beyond the call of duty. Supreme Court Justice Yvonne Kauger helped above and beyond the call of her office. And Mary Pointer, my banker, knows only three words which she repeats over and over again, "Write the book." "Write the book." "Write the book."

Others who helped me along life's way include Tom Adler, Andy Coats, Bob Macy, and George Short.

Among the physicians and ophthalmologists who helped save my life and vision are Drs. Charles Bethea, James Hartsuck, Tom Acers, Tom Aaberg, Sterling Baker, Jim Little, and Stan Muenzler.

Finally, it's time to pay tribute to my wife of forty-eight years, Caroline Cannon. She has stood by me in times of turmoil and trouble, taken care of me when I was sick and in bed, and typed the raw manuscript from my rambling musings and scribblings.

§ § §

Index of Names